# Travel Tips For Visiting Southeast Asia

Cora .F Riddle

# Introduction

Embark on an unforgettable journey through the enchanting lands of Vietnam, Laos, and Cambodia with this book. This package encompasses the ultimate travel guides for each of these mesmerizing destinations, providing you with essential insights, tips, and recommendations to make your trip a truly remarkable experience.

Our Ultimate Vietnam Travel Guide is your passport to Vietnam's rich culture, history, and natural beauty. We'll help you navigate the vibrant streets of Vietnam, offering valuable advice on accommodations, transportation, and the delectable cuisine that awaits you. Explore must-see cultural sights, get your adrenaline pumping with exciting activities, and discover the country's nightlife. Your Vietnam bucket list will come to life with the help of our expert recommendations.

In the Ultimate Laos Travel Guide, you'll dive into the heart of Laos, uncovering its unique cuisine and natural wonders. Find the perfect places to stay, learn about transportation options, and embark on a culinary adventure through Lao cuisine. Discover Laos' captivating sights, indulge in exciting activities, and experience the country's nightlife scene. Our Laos bucket list will guide you on an unforgettable journey.

Lastly, the Ultimate Cambodia Travel Guide invites you to explore the mesmerizing temples of Angkor and the wonders of Cambodia. We'll help you choose accommodations, provide transportation insights, and introduce you to Cambodia's culinary delights. Explore must-see sights, engage in thrilling activities, and experience the vibrant nightlife of Cambodia's top cities. With our Cambodia bucket list, you'll create memories to last a lifetime.

Each travel guide in this package is a gateway to a world of adventure and discovery. Whether you're a cultural enthusiast, a culinary explorer, or an adrenaline seeker, this book will ensure that you have the tools and knowledge to make the most of your journey through Vietnam, Laos, and Cambodia.

Get ready to embark on an extraordinary adventure in South-East Asia.

# Contents

# The Ultimate Vietnam Travel Guide

*How To Get The Most Out Of Your Travel Through Vietnam From North To South*

# Map Of Vietnam

# Let's Get Started!

You just have downloaded the book, "The Ultimate Vietnam Travel Guide: How To Get The Most Out Of Your Travel Through Vietnam From North To South".

I am excited to hear that you either want to visit or are planning your visit to Vietnam.

This book will give you a short but comprehensive guide on how you can enjoy your holiday or travel to the fullest.

Vietnam is a beautiful, exotic country and it is very much worthwhile to visit. I understand that when you do go, you'd want to plan your destinations and activities as much as you can. However, the resources that are available today contain so much information; it is difficult to go through it all.

That is why I created this 30-minute read that will provide you enough resources to plan your trip. All the topics that are necessary for a fulfilled stay are included. The book includes chapters like: the type of accommodation that is available for you to all the transportation options you can use and much more. It will be like I'm holding your hand while guiding you through this miraculous country.

In fact, I have personally guided some of my friends through the cities of North as well as South Vietnam. Growing up in a western country while being from Vietnamese descent, I have lived between both cultures. Therefore, this easy to digest guide will let you experience the Vietnamese culture while keeping a western perspective in mind. The inside tips you're about to discover will guide you to make the most out of your trip.

Let's get started and I hope you'll enjoy this beautiful trip!

# Vietnamese Culture and Customs

Whenever you're traveling in a foreign country, there are new customs to learn. Vietnam is no different. By gaining a basic understanding before you go, you'll find that you can integrate into the culture a little better. It's also helpful to avoid offending anyone, though Vietnamese people tend to be quite laid back and friendly.

As you travel, you'll probably notice quite a few differences between your own culture and the Vietnamese culture. Embrace the differences! You have the perfect chance to learn about another country as you travel and interact with the locals.

Face is a concept that is quite common in Asian countries. While it doesn't translate correctly to English, the overall idea is that it affects someone's dignity or honor and reputation. Publicly humiliating or scolding another person can cause them to lose face. Likewise, compliments can give face. Pay attention to how people around you act and you should pick this concept up fairly rapidly.

When a group of people is together in Vietnam, the oldest members are greeted first and given respect for their status. Keep this in mind when meeting new people.

A few things to keep in mind include avoiding the following:

- Public kissing or other displays of affection

- Touching people's heads or shoulders or passing something over their head.

- Wearing shorts in public, apart from at the beach.

- Crossing your arms.

- Pointing.

Each of these can be offensive, but it's easy enough to avoid potential issues.

As in many countries, it's customary to bring a gift if you are invited to dinner at someone's home. However, a Vietnamese host will often refuse the gift the first time, to avoid appearing greedy. You should continue to offer the gift until it is accepted. Good dinner guest gifts include liquor, flowers, fruit or incense.

Of course, dining requires a certain amount of etiquette, as well. Most meals are family-style, so it is a very comfortable environment. The oldest at the table are seated and served first, so if you are younger, wait for them. You can usually watch everyone else at the table to see what is expected of you, but keep a few things in mind.

First, never stick your chopsticks upright in a bowl of rice. When you're done eating, you can lay them across the top of the bowl. You should also avoid eating steadily and make sure to lay down your chopsticks to take a little break from time to time. It's considered polite to make conversation during a meal.

Anytime you are expected anywhere, try to be punctual. It is rather rude to show up late for a meal or meeting.

Many of these are fairly common sense. Make sure you respect others and greet the oldest person in a group first. Keep your eyes open and you'll find that it is pretty easy to pick up on local customs. Vietnamese are friendly and open and tend to be quite happy to share their culture with foreigners, so it shouldn't be too difficult to learn new things.

# Where To Stay For A Fair Price

Having a roof over your head is one of the first things you'll want to plan for when

Having a roof over your head is one of the first things you'll want to plan for when traveling. Once you know where you're staying, you can begin to expand your travel plans.

Your budget and interests will determine the type of accommodation you can enjoy while in Vietnam. There are plenty of options, from luxury hotels to home stays. Accommodation is quite affordable throughout the country, so even if you are on a tight budget, you can find a great place to stay.

Hotels are the first place most travelers look to when they need to sleep. Similar to the standard of international traveler, hotels range from small rooms with one bed and a shared bathroom to luxurious suites in high-end hotels. While you do get what you pay for, you'll find that prices are quite reasonable. Low budget rooms often run for $10 a night, while a nicer place will cost between $25-50 a night.

Don't be surprised if you are asked to leave your key at the front desk when leaving a hotel for the day. This is common practice in many guesthouses and ensures that you will not lose your key while out and about.

Booking.com and Hotels.com are two good resources for pre-arranging your hotel room.

For the budget traveler, hostels provide a very low cost place to stay. In most hostels, you will be bunking in a dorm room for a few dollars a night. Some hostels also offer private rooms for a little higher fee and there is a communal kitchen where you can prepare your own meals.

For the outgoing backpacker, a hostel can be a place to meet others traveling in the same direction, pick up tips for nearby sights and learn about off-the-beaten-path must sees.

You can pre-book hostels on Hostel World, where you will find some of the most popular places to stay around Vietnam. Hostels.com and Hostelbookers are other good resource for travelers.

When you stay at a hostel, make sure to take care of your belongings. You can either use their lockers (bring your own lock) or sometimes they allow you to store belongings at the receptionist' desk.

As with anywhere in the world, some areas of Vietnam's popular tourist destinations are better for staying in than others. Unless you've talked to locals before you arrive, it can be pretty difficult to guess where you should and should not go.

The ideal hotel or hostel will be located near sights you want to see, or, at the very least, near good transportation. In Sapa, try to find a hotel like Sapa Eden Hotel, near the Market Area. This is close to plenty of sights and will give you easy access to tasty street food. Another option is the City Center, where you'll be near the hustle and bustle of downtown.

Hanoi, with all its many sights to see can be a bit confusing, but if you're looking for a nice, pleasant area with plenty of restaurants and shopping spots, Hoan Kiem District is a good option. This is located near the center of the Old Quarter, an excellent place if you're trying to stay on a tight budget. The Hanoi Serendipity Hotel is a clean, pleasant place to stay in this area, or check New Vision Hostel nearby. There are plenty of cafes and booking agents throughout the Old Quarter, plus you can walk to some very interesting tourist spots. Transport can be had to other areas of Hanoi when you're ready to check out some of the more distant places of interest.

Ho Chi Minh City is large enough to warrant a few "top" areas to stay in. District 1 is usually the most popular among those just arriving in country. The hotels here are close to the airport and offer a range of prices for all budgets. If you're looking for cheaper places to stay, the western section of District 1 is your best option, near D Pham Ngu Lao. The hottest bars and clubs, however, are to the east, near D Dong Khoi, but be aware that you'll pay a premium to stay there. New Saigon Hostel and Galaxy Hotel & Capsule are two very affordable places to stay in this area of the city.

Some areas don't give you much choice as to where you should stay. Ha Long Bay, for example, has its best accommodations along the beach. Mui Ne is a similar town, with most hotels and hostels lined up along the seafront. Here, a good choice is Mui Ne Backpacker Village, which is affordable and well rated.

If you really want to experience life as a local, there is no better way to immerse in the Vietnamese culture than by staying with a local family. You will be free to explore the region you are staying in, but will also experience life as how locals do. Most home stays offer a separate bedroom and you will share the living space with the rest of the family. Meals are often provided, which can be a great opportunity to try new foods.

Interested in learning the language? Living with a family for a few weeks will hone your skills. While most hosts speak English, they will be happy to practice with you after language classes. Depending on the host, you may have access to amenities like a pool, bicycles and Internet.

Homestay.com is a good place to start looking for a host in Vietnam. There are homestays offered in the larger cities, like *Hanoi* and *Ho Chi Minh City*, but there are also homes scattered throughout more remote areas. From accommodation in the center of a city to a room overlooking rice paddies, each host family offers something different.

Hotels and hostels can get old after a while and many people long for the comforts of home. A vacation house gives you a whole home to enjoy, for a few nights or as long as a month. These rentals are meant to be short term, so you don't have to worry about yearlong leases.

To find homes for rent, try AirBnB, a booking site that makes it simple to rent directly from the owner of the home. You can book as few or as many nights as you want and the homes are already furnished and equipped. You can find a home for as little as $15 a person, or pay more for a larger house.

## Taking Local Advice

If you aren't one to plan ahead, you may find it beneficial to talk to some locals upon arrival in the city you plan to stay in. They will be able to point you to affordable accommodation in the area.

No matter which city you are in, you'll find a range of options for laying your head. From sharing a dorm with other travelers or hanging out with a host family to sleeping in a nice hotel or renting an entire home, you have plenty of great options.

# Getting Around In And Out Of The City

Vietnam may not be a huge country, but it is packed with incredible places to visit. You'll need to get from town to town and there are quite a few transportation options to choose from. Try as many as you can to really enjoy the experience.

Within the cities, you have several options, including xe om, cyclos and xe lams. Xe om roughly translates to "hugging car" and it is much like it sounds. You sit behind the driver on a motorcycle and hang on to the driver. Make sure you set a price for your destination before you head out. This will give you an up close and personal look at the traffic in major cities around Vietnam. This is a great option if you want to get around in the city.

Cyclos are essentially tricycles with a seat for a passenger in front. The driver sits behind you and peddles the cyclo. They are not permitted in many areas of *Ho Chi Minh City* or *Hanoi*, but you will find them just about everywhere else. Nowadays, the cyclo is more used as a tourist attraction in cities like *Hue* and *Hoi An*. Make sure to negotiate your ride before hopping on!

A xe lam is a fun way to get around when you only need to travel a short distance. A motorcycle powers these unique vehicles up front, but the back end is similar to a small truck with two wheels. Passengers sit in the back section and the driver rides the motorcycle up front.

## DIY Transport

Not everyone wants to be dependent on public transportation systems. If you would prefer to manage your own transport, you can choose to get around on your own.

A good option, if you want to get some exercise, is a bicycle. Many hotels offer bicycle rentals, but you can also purchase one if you are planning on being in country for a while. This is the easiest way for a foreigner to get around the hectic cities

Bicycles are a common sight in Vietnam and you can easily store them on top of a bus or in a train's cargo car if you prefer to try another transportation method.

It can be very difficult to drive a car in the big cities if you aren't used to the unique traffic patterns. Fortunately, if you rent a vehicle, most companies include a driver.

Motorcycles are cheap and easier to weave in and out of traffic. Drivers are available if you aren't brave enough to attempt this on your own. Mopeds and scooters are the cheapest option. Be aware that you'll drive at your own risks and should be careful. Make sure to check with your travel insurance whether they would reimburse, in case something happens.

If you are not confident about your driving skills, you should only rent a motorcycle in the less crowded cities like *Mui Ne* and *Da Nang*. If you happen to be pulled over by a cop for not wearing a helmet or driving in a one-way traffic, always speak English and NEVER say the word money. Usually they will let you go without paying, because they won't understand you and they don't want to waste their time. However, if you'd mention the word money, they'll understand that and won't let you go unless you hand over a couple of notes. So be aware!

## Traveling Long Distances

Getting from one part of the country to another requires more than just a taxi. Fortunately, it isn't difficult to travel longer distances.

Probably the best option for long distance travel is a bus. Buses run to every corner of Vietnam. The express buses are the most expensive options, though they get you to your destination quickly. You can buy your ticket before leaving at the appropriate bus stop in the city you are in. Foreigners usually pay more than locals.

Vietnam Railways manages train system throughout the country. This is probably the most comfortable way to travel, but it is certainly not the fastest. If you worry about having not enough time, plan to travel by night, because there are different options on a train. When you do decide to go by train, you should book in advance, because the nice compartments tend to be sold out very fast, since they aren't too expensive compared to the regular compartments.

There are four classes to travel in on the trains, but air conditioning is only available on express trains.

**Hard Seat:** The hard bench seats in this class are very uncomfortable after a few hours.

**Soft Seat:** These seats are covered in vinyl and are more comfortable for long trips.

**Hard Sleeper:** Each compartment offers two bunk beds with three levels of beds. The top bunk is the cheapest, with the bottom being the most expensive.

**Soft Sleeper:** This is the most luxurious option with two bunk beds (four beds total) per compartment. All bunks cost the same.

Meals are included in the ticket price, but you'll want to bring some snacks yourself or purchase them from the vendors at each station.

Boats are a popular method of travel between the islands of *Halong Bay* and *Nha Trang*. The Mekong River is another area where you can use boats as transportation to travel up and down the river or its tributaries. There are also ferries that cross the rivers throughout the country.

Enjoy the adventure of getting around the country. It's certainly an exciting part of the experience that is Vietnam.

Boats are a popular method of travel between the islands of *Halong Bay* and *Nha Trang*. The Mekong River is another area where you can use boats as transportation to travel up and down the river or its tributaries. There are also ferries that cross the rivers throughout the country.

# What To Eat On And Off The Streets

Eating is a big part of any trip and Vietnam has a lot to offer in terms of unique food. Many travelers stick to the more expensive restaurants, but the street stalls are where the real flavor is at. Not only is this food cheap, it's also amazingly tasty and certainly worth trying.

Mealtimes are somewhat earlier than Westerners might expect throughout the country. Lunch, for example, is often between 10:30 - 11, so it's best to eat then to get the freshest food.

## Where to Find the Best Food in Each City

In *Hanoi*, head to the Old Quarter and find Hang Vai Street. This is a bamboo shop street, but near the end, you'll discover a wealth of pho shops and sugar cane juice stands. There are plenty of street vendors here, as well, selling some of the best food in the city. Definitely try some pho here, a simple noodle dish that is different at every stand. The base is a broth with rice noodles, but meat (beef and chicken are most popular) and herbs are usually added.

Another street to check out in Hanoi is Mai Hắc Đế street, packed with delicious food shops and stands.

*Ho Chi Minh City* also has its famous food street. Banh xeo is sold on Đinh Công Tráng street, so head there if you want to try the different variations of this dish. While in *Ho Chi Minh City*, look for the street that is dedicated to cho ca, a <u>delightful dish</u> of fried fish bits with ginger, dill, turmeric and garlic. The fried fish is extremely popular among the locals.

**Restaurants:** Vietnam is home to many good restaurants. Order your food from a menu (it's helpful to have a <u>cheat sheet of food vocabulary</u>) and pay at the end of your meal. Dishes are usually meant to be shared between a few people. International restaurants are readily available in the larger cities.

Soups are an essential part of Vietnamese cuisine and are found in most restaurants. The one-plate shops frequently specialize in a soup. If you're in need of some warming, bun bo hue with vermicelli is a good choice. It's essentially a sturdier version of pho. The broth is beef, but the meat are usually chunks of pork. Lemongrass and cilantro add a distinct flavor.

Ga tan, the Vietnamese version of chicken soup, this tasty street food is full of fresh herbs and chunks of chicken. The soup is green and you may not recognize all the chicken bits that are cooked in it, but it is almost guaranteed to keep colds away. You should also try bun bo nam bo. A broth-less noodle soup, bun bo nam bo is a quick and easy dish to find. The noodles are topped with thin strips of beef, peanuts and bean sprouts and mixed with plenty of fresh herbs. A little fish sauce and chili pepper give the noodles some kick.

If you're not interested in soup, don't worry. There are other options, like banh xeo. This crisp crepe is stuffed with shrimp, bean sprouts and pork, plus plenty of fresh herbs. Banh xeo is served with a dipping sauce, which varies depending on the chef. It's acceptable to cut your crepe into pieces for easier handling so you can dip it. Try wrapping lettuce or rice paper around the crepe to hold it together. Banh xeo is not sold in the north, so enjoy it while you're in *Ho Chi Minh City*.

For lunch, try a crusty baguette, filled with a wide range of goodies. It's called banh mi and is the ideal lunchtime sandwich in Vietnam. You'll find pickled carrots and radishes, herbs, barbecued pork, liver paste, cucumber, green onion, chili and ham smashed between the two pieces of bread.

You should also try rau muong. Made with morning glory, this dish is heavy on the garlic and is often served with beer. It's a delicious; stir-fried meal that everyone will enjoy. Look for the dish in *Hanoi* beer gardens or small restaurants.

Banana flower salad, or nom hoa chuoi is an interesting combination of green papaya, chicken, fish sauce, peanuts, carrots and banana flowers. The end result is a somewhat salty salad that tastes fresh and crisp, a refreshing choice for a light lunch.

Many restaurants serve goi cuon, or spring rolls. Goi cuon is stuffed with greens, a bit of seafood or pork and dipped in fish or peanut sauce to eat. Don't expect your usual fried spring rolls; these are surprisingly light and absolutely delectable.

Everyone visiting the country needs to take a trip to Hoi An to try cao lau. Thick noodles are mixed into broth with pork, herbs and crispy wontons to make this delicious dish. The real stuff is found in *Hoi An* and is made with water only found in the Ba Le well. If it's not made with Ba Le water, it's not considered authentic.

## Street Stalls

Eating in the street can be quite the culinary experience, but it pays to be careful. Look for stalls that are crowded, indicating that they are popular. It's also best to go to a dedicated food market.

If you're feeling peckish, look for a street cart that sells banh khot, or mini pancakes. They're not the usual pancakes, however. These Vietnamese pancakes are stuffed with shrimp and mung beans with a flavoring of spring onions. The outside is crunchy from the coconut milk. While the pancakes are tiny, just a bite each, they are a fun snack.

Found in street stalls, bot chien is a favorite after school snack, as well as a tasty treat after a night of partying. Fried rice flour dough with a fried egg is served with a mix of papaya, green onions, rice vinegar and green onions.

Herbs are a vital part of banh uot thit nuong. It's full of cilantro, basil, mint, lemongrass and chili, all of which lend the grilled pork a light, healthy taste. The entire mixture, along with sugar, salt and some fish sauce, is encased in rice paper and eaten as rolls.

Bun cha is one of the most popular lunch options available in the cities, particularly Ho Chi Minh City. Marinated pork is formed into small patties and then grilled. The process releases a heavenly scent that is pretty hard to miss. The meat patties are served with broth, rice noodles, fish sauce and herbs. You can also buy banh bao wherever pork is sold on the street.

You'll find these rather non-traditional pork buns for sale by vendors walking with their wares. Check Hanoi's Old Quarter for some of the best buns. They are stuffed with pork meat and some even contain a tasty quail egg in the middle.

Vietnamese food also provides plenty of options to satisfy your sweet tooth. If you're in the mood for something sweet, che is a refreshing choice. Usually served in a bowl or a glass, you will find the layers of coconut milk, ice, fruit and bean jelly to be tasty and cooling on a hot day. Banh tet is another tasty dessert choice, though finding these little rice cakes can be tough unless you're in Vietnam during Tét, the Vietnamese New Year. Savory sticky rice is filled with mung bean paste and wrapped in banana leaves for sale in the street. The dessert versions contain a sweeter red bean and banana filling.

Another great choice on a hot day is hoa qua dam. Fresh fruit is chopped into a cup and mixed with sweetened condensed milk in this street food favorite. You can also get it with just shaved ice, but the condensed milk is all part of the experience.

Sweet drinks are also the norm and can be found in both restaurants and street stalls. Ca phe trung or "egg coffee" is a favorite of both locals and tourists. The coffee in this drink is minimal, topped with egg white foam that is sweet and creamy. Café Vietnam is a sweet drink that packs a punch with strong coffee and condensed milk in one cup. Some places serve it mixed, while others offer two layers. The coffee is served hot or cold, after a meal.

There are hundreds of other foods that are worthy of tasting, but the best way to learn about them is to simply head out to the nearest food market and start taste testing. You will find plenty of new favorite dishes.

## DIY Food: When You Want Make Your Own

Don't forget to hit the market! You may prefer to do some cooking on your own, which means you will need to shop for ingredients. This can be an adventure in itself, as you head to the local market. Here you will find a wide range of unfamiliar fruits and vegetables, as well as familiar ones.

Being adventurous helps when purchasing your own food. You can negotiate prices in the market; so don't pay the first asking price. Look for the freshest product and don't be afraid to move on if it's not what you are looking for.

# Festivals in Vietnam

While Vietnam is fascinating all on its own, you won't want to miss a festival if you're around when one is going on. Vietnamese people are friendly and often more than happy to include you in their celebrations. I highly recommend spending some time with the locals, especially if you have a chance to join in on the celebration.

## January/February

The Giong Festival is celebrated on different days throughout the first lunar month of the year. The actual date depends on the area that the festival is held, since each temple has a different festival day throughout Hanoi. You can find celebrations and ceremonies at Soc Temple, Phu Dong Temple, and several others, to celebrate Saint Giong. The festival includes folk games and performances including a depiction of Saint Giong's battle.

Tet, or the Vietnamese New Year, is a big event that is certainly worth checking out. It is a multi-day celebration that involves decorating homes, plenty of food and visiting ancestors. This holiday is the same as the Chinese New Year and it is customary to give gifts of food. You'll see dragon dances in the streets, so this is a great time to visit the country.

## March

On the sixth day of the second lunar month, Hai Ba Trung Day is celebrated. This holiday focuses on the Trung Sisters who rose up against the Chinese back in 40 AD. It's an interesting celebration, though not necessarily one to travel to Vietnam for.

Thanh Minh or the Holiday of the Dead is celebrated in March. People pay their respects to those who have gone before, by visiting graves and leaving gifts. Common gifts are food or flowers, but incense may also be left on the graves, which are cleaned and beautified before the festival.

## April

On April 30<sup>th</sup>, the Liberation Day of South Vietnam (also known as Reunification Day) is celebrated. This marks the day in 1975 when the North Vietnamese army was victorious. You'll see the city streets decorated with flags and banners, as well as special lights. Depending on the city, there will be various parades and shows going on before and on the actual day. Get to the main streets of the bigger cities (especially Ho Chi Minh City) nice and early to see the parades.

Another interesting festival held in April is the Elephant Racing Festival. Head to Tay Nguyen to see the elephants and festival attendees dressed in brilliant clothing. Elephants are well fed and rested ahead of time and then brought from surrounding villages to Ban Don. The races are held throughout the day, with the winners being fed sugar cane and bananas. While some races take place on land, there is also a swimming competition and several elephant games. Later, the humans take over with dancing, eating and drinking.

You may also want to check out Le Mat, a small village in Long Bien District, near Hanoi. They hold a snake festival each April on the 23<sup>rd</sup> day of the third lunar month to celebrate the snake catching profession. There's a water procession to take pond water to the temple, an offering at the temple and snake competitions, as well as snake wine to drink.

## May

Doan Ngu or Summer Soltice is celebrated on the fifth day of the fifth lunar month. During this time, people make offerings to the spirits to keep disease away and encourage good health for the future.

Also in May (or occasionally April) is Halong's Tourism Week. This is a great time to hang out at Halong and see some of the local traditions. This is a fairly new festival, debuting for real in 2012, but it is a lot of fun! You'll find food festivals, art exhibitions and sporting competitions, as well as performances in dance and theater.

## June/July

Children's Day is celebrated on June first each year. While some people celebrate in a family, it is also a day celebrated by groups. Children are given plenty of attention and are officially out of school, so they are taken on picnics, walks or spend time at a playground. Parties are also common in daycares and residential groups. However, there is also a charitable side to the holiday, where donations are collected to help kids who need it, as well as visits to local pediatric wards.

Also early in June is the Parasite Killing Festival. This may sound rather odd and possibly unpleasant, but it's actually a very beneficial celebration. Held on the fifth day of the fifth lunar month, Tet Doan Ngo involves picking herbs at the moment when the sun is the highest it will be in the sky. Picking the leaves is a communal event. These, along with sour foods like rice wine and lemons, are eaten to cleanse the digestive tract. Offerings are also given to spirits.

## August/September

Late August or early September is when the people of Do Son District celebrate the Water Goddess with a buffalo fighting festival. This is truly a unique celebration, so if you are in Haiphong City during this time, check it out.

The festival includes buffalo fights between carefully trained buffalo, as well as offerings to the spirits. There are also processions and a variety of activities that you can enjoy, including dance competitions and games. The winning animals are sacrificed at the end of the festival, bringing good luck to the buffalo's home town.

## December

The Kmer celebrate Ooc Om Boc in the tenth month of the lunar year, on the day of the full moon. Head to the nearest Khmer area to celebrate the moon festival. At midnight, offerings of fruit and sticky rice are offered up to the moon to promote good weather and crops for the coming year. There is also a ghe boat race, dancing, music and workshops on farming practices. Foreigners are often welcomed.

There are many celebrations that are held in individual towns, as well. Many of these are quite small, but if you are in the area, it's worth checking them out. Talk to your host family or the hotel owners where you're staying to learn more about the events occurring while you are there. You might be surprised to hear about some fun that isn't even mentioned in guides like this one.

# Must See Cultural Sights Around Vietnam

Vietnam is rich in both culture and history. You could literally spend months exploring the country and still not see everything there is to see. History has been preserved in many forms here, from elaborate monuments to historical buildings that have been carefully maintained over the years.

## Exploring Vietnam's History

There is much more to Vietnam than the war, but you'll find a number of sights dedicated to this period of history. These include the War Remnants Museum in *Ho Chi Minh City* and the Cu Chi Tunnels.

The Cu Chi Tunnels are located around an hour from *Ho Chi Minh City* and are worth a visit. The Viet Cong dug these tunnels during the war, so they could move around in safety under the ground. Visitors can now view models of the tunnels or even explore them, if they're not claustrophobic. Here is an interesting documentary on the tunnels.

Reaching even further back into the country's history, you'll find a number of temple sites in the area. My Son Temple is a group of abandoned Hindu temple ruins. They were originally built to Shiva somewhere between the 4th-14th century AD.

The temples can be found north of Da Nang, settled in a little valley. Take a taxi or a motorbike ride to the site and enjoy wandering about. The local Champa, who originally built the temples, perform dances sometimes on the site, so get there early.

The Hun Pagoda at Thien Tu Phuc Monastery is in the Chi Linh District. Originally built during the 13th century, this pagoda has been restored several times and has been expanded considerably over the years. It is well worth visiting since the temple features over 80 rooms with nearly 400 statues. Behind the pagoda is an ancestor house where you'll find images of famous ancestors here.

Another impressive temple is Chua Huong or the Perfume Pagoda. Not too far south from Hanoi, this beautiful temple is home to some very lovely scenery, as well as multiple pagodas and cave shrines. Built along Huong Son or Perfume Mount, the temple stretches right to the top. There is a large cavern that serves as the center of the temple complex, making it well worth a trip out.

Located in Hue, the Imperial City was the capital city of Vietnam in 1802 and is a must-see part of the country. It was considered to be the cultural and religious heart of the country until 1945. The area is quite picturesque and well worth visiting. The architecture is amazing and ideal for taking photos. You'll learn a lot about the past of Vietnam through this site.

Much of the Imperial City was damaged in 1968. Many of the buildings have been restored, but those that were too badly damaged are now turned over to rice paddies.

Also in *Hanoi* is the Mausoleum of Mr. Ho Chi Minh, credited with the founding of modern Vietnam. You can see his mummified corpse in a glass sarcophagus in the depths of his elegant mausoleum made of marble. This is a very special monument for those who live here, so take care to respect tradition and stay quiet and respectful while in the mausoleum.

Ho Chi Minh City is where most people spend the majority of their time in the country. While you're there, check out the Saigon Central Post Office. While a post office may seem like a strange choice for a tourist site, this one is well worth checking out. It took five years to build the impressive building. It was finished in 1891. Located across the street from the Notre Dame Cathedral in Ho Chi Minh City, there are plenty of photo opportunities to be had. You can head inside even if you have no official business (the post office is fully functional to this day).

Don't forget the Saigon Notre Dame Basilica. This amazing cathedral is a draw for tourists and locals, with its dual spires and spacious interior. The impressive architecture is the result of a design competition. The cathedral was built by French colonists and the current version was begun in 1877 and continued under construction until 1880, though the bell towers were added nearly 15 years later. The original building is entirely made from imported French materials, though upgrades have been made with local bricks and tiles.

There is a statue of the Our Lady of Peace in the cathedral, once rumored to have shed tears. The rumor caused clergy from the Catholic Church to examine the statue. Though the end decision was that the statue had not cried, people continued to watch it.

Not far from Hoan Kiem Lake in Hanoi, you'll find the Temple of Literature. This temple, built in 1070 and dedicated to Confucius, has a brilliant past. Not only was it a temple, it is also the site of the first university in the country, founded just six years after the temple was built. Nobles studied here, though anyone with the right qualifications was admitted after 1442.

The Temple of Literature features a number of stelae that still stand from the many, which were placed to keep track of the best scholars. Inside the temple, there are beautiful formal gardens and the Well of Heavenly Clarity, a large pond in a square shape.

Venture further south to Da Lat to find even more historical and cultural monuments. While this is a fairly young city in comparison to most others in the area, Da Lat is a fascinating place to visit. Here, you can check out the emperor's throne room, bedroom and office in Bao Dai's Summer Palace. This is one of the reasons the town is known as a party town, since Bao Dai used to travel there to live it up. There are three buildings that make up the palace, but not all of it is open to the public.

If you do visit the summer palace, make note of the art and sculptures, as well as the original furniture and décor that is still in use. You're not allowed to take pictures inside, so commit it all to memory!

On a slightly more bizarre note, don't miss the Crazy House. While certainly not historical, this oddly tree-like building makes up much of the culture in Da Lat and is worth a visit. The sculpted house is full of tunnels and ladders to lead to different areas of the building, where various statues and pieces of art are housed. It serves as a guesthouse and an art gallery for those bold enough to enter.

Finally, check out the historic Da Lat train station with its wood steam train. Ride down the track to Trai Mat and back. You have to have at least four people to ride, however, so start collecting tourists if you want to do the loop.

## Exploring Vietnam's Wilder Side

The Marble Mountains offer several caves to explore, but the main interest is the main cave, where a carved Buddha sits in a stream of daylight. There are plenty of pagodas and grottos throughout the area, as well as a large number of vendors. You can take a lift up or climb the many stairs to reach the caves, just outside of Da Nang.

The Marble Mountains tend to have a large number of tours streaming through them, so you're better off going at dawn or later in the day. The site is open throughout daylight hours, but most tourists head up later in the morning and afternoon.

The heart of Hanoi is built around Huan Kiem Lake. This body of water has been a special part of the city's past and is a unique color that is not found easily in other Vietnamese lakes. The lake is also full of tortoises, which are considered to be sacred animals. You may even be lucky enough to check out one of the huge creatures in the water. Thanks to their presence, Huan Kiem Lake is considered a sacred place.

For those adventurers interested in getting a closer look at Vietnam's more rural lifestyle, a trip to Viet Hai Village is a must. It's not easy to get to, but the village has only been exposed to the outside world for a handful of years. The villagers here still live a very self-sufficient life and it is worth the long hike and boat trip through the jungle to find this little piece of heaven. To get there, you take a boat from Catba to Viet Hai Harbor. From there, you can walk or cycle down a dirt road to the community, which is roughly six kilometers from the harbor.

Once you arrive, you'll find yourself surrounded by thatch cottages, with people tending their crops in the fields. It's a peaceful atmosphere and there are plenty of hiking trails around the area.

Near the Vietnam-China border in the northwestern part of the country, you'll find Sapa, a community based on farming. However, since the terrain here is so steep, the rice is grown on terraces cut into the mountain, rather than flat paddies.

You can tour the area and check out the impressive terracing, where corn and other vegetables are also cultivated, apart from the rice. For anyone interested in agriculture in Vietnam, this is a fascinating place to visit. At 1,500 feet above sea level, Sapa is surrounded by mountains, including the tallest peak in Vietnam, Fansipan. While the area is quickly becoming better known, it's still well worth a visit to take a look at the area, do some hiking and meet the friendly people of the hill tribes.

Due to the altitude and mountains, expect some rain while you're in Sapa. It often cycles through several types of weather in a day, making it impossible to predict when you will need a rain poncho or boots.

Rice farming is a way of life outside the bustling cities and if alternatively, visitors will find rice paddies are a charming place to relax. Head to the *Mekong Delta* to take a ferry over to *My Hoa Hung islet* where you can enjoy a homestay and visit the rice paddies for yourself. Visitors are encouraged to participate in the daily life of the area, farming alongside the locals and sharing meals with their hosts.

Rice paddy tours are available in *Hoi An*, as well as other areas where rice farming is prolific. These include a guide and transportation. You'll also be introduced to the farmers that work the paddies.

Farming may be found inland, but there is plenty of activity on the coast, as well. Anyone who enjoys fishing will enjoy the coast of Vietnam. You don't need a fishing permit here and you can just arrange with a local fisherman to go out on the ocean. Most fishing takes place with traditional equipment such as nets and handmade poles, so if you want anything else, you'll have to book a tour or bring your own.

Sea fishing is best between *Phan Tiet* and *Quy Nhon*, near the center of the country's coastline. There are a number of small resort towns in this stretch of coast and tour companies abound. You can also head out on the *Mekong Delta* and join a mud-fishing tour if you want to try catching fish by hand.

A relaxing way to see more of the country is on a cruise. You can take a short day trip around *Ha Long Bay*, or enjoy a 2-3 day cruise on a larger boat. Travel companies offer a range of options for the interested traveler. If you take a smaller boat, you can rent it just for your group.

Mud baths are said to rejuvenate your entire body and help you look young again. Take a taxi from *Nha Trang* if you want to experience the messy fun for yourself. For less than $20, you can get a premium ticket that gives you 20 minutes in an egg shaped mud bath and unlimited access to the Jacuzzi, spa and sauna.

100 Egg Mud Baths is more than just mud and water, though. You can explore the beautiful grounds, have a cookout or hang out at one of several cafes and restaurants on the grounds. There's even rock climbing and massages available, so it makes a good activity for a day trip.

If you're interested in taking some of the local culture home with you, taking a cooking class is a great way to do just that. You can find cooking classes throughout Vietnam, so there will be one in the area you are visiting.

Hanoi Cooking Centre, in Hanoi, is a well-regarded place to learn if you are in the area. The center offers local cooking classes, as well as international ones. There's even a class for kids if you're traveling with family.

Hoi An has the Morning Glory Cooking School, which serves as a restaurant, as well as a school. In Ho Chi Minh City, you can attend one of several different classes at the Vietnam Cookery Center. They offer tourist programs, extended programs and even chef classes.

There's no shortage of fun to be hand in this beautiful country, but if you are ready for a little more excitement, let's move on.

# Where to Get Your Adrenaline Rush

If museums aren't your cup of tea, you might want to try some of the more extreme sports available. You can get quite the adrenaline rush if you know where to look.

Before you start risking your life, make sure your travel insurance covers extreme sports. Not all policies do and you could be in trouble if you injure yourself.

Water sports are a popular way to enjoy the warm ocean and both foreigners and locals partake. Try your hand at jet skiing in *Nha Trang*. Head to the beach and you'll find rentals along the waterfront. It's a good idea to check your equipment and even take some photos before renting to ensure you don't get charged for equipment that was already damaged.

With steady winds and calm seas, *Mui Ne Bay* is the ideal place to enjoy kitesurfing. Extreme Sports Café offers lessons and equipment rental for those ready to try their hand at skimming across the water.

Diving is another excellent way to spend some time in on the coast. The most popular areas include *Hoi An, Phu Quoc, Whale Island, Nha Trang*

and *Con Dao*. Each of these areas is serviced by <u>Rainbow Divers</u>. You can take PADI courses or simply rent the equipment and a boat to go out in a small group. There are also night dives and specialty dives available.

Once you're ready to dry off, try some of the other extreme sports available throughout the country. Soaring over the sea or jungle can be an exciting experience. <u>Paragliding</u> may be done in tandem with a qualified pilot, or you can go for it on your own, if you are certified. Inland flights are available near *Da Lat*, where you launch from *Lang Biang Mountain* and fly over rice paddies. *Mui Ne* offers paragliding options near the ocean.

Also in Da Lat, you can try riding an elephant. Take a tour from the town to Prenn Waterfall to check out this fun experience. While the falls themselves are not particularly impressive, you can trek the walkway that runs behind the falling water for a unique experience. The really interesting part, however, is riding an elephant through the jungle on a short sightseeing tour.

There are also a number of well-trained ostriches at the falls, which you can ride. It might be fun to try, just so you can say you did!

If you want to experience something rather unique, you should head to *Mui Ne* for sandboarding. Here, you'll find tall white sand dunes near the town and red dunes further away. You can rent plastic sleds in both locations, to slide down the dunes with. The white dunes are more popular, but also a little safer.

Taking a <u>quad or ATV</u> into the sand dunes at *Mui Ne* can also be an interesting experience. It beats hiking the dunes and you'll get a chance to see far more of the area than you would on foot. While renting a quad is pricey ($35 per hour), it is still the most exhilarating way to see the desert.

Whether you enjoy diving deep in the ocean or prefer to stay high in the air, Vietnam caters to all adventurers.

# The Places to Be During The Nighttime

The nightlife in the large cities of Vietnam is a little different than most. While clubs and bars are around, most of them close before midnight. *Ho Chi Minh City* is a good place to head to if you like clubbing. *Hanoi* has its hot spots, but is generally quieter and has less to offer in terms of nightlife, though it is by no means dead.

## Bars and Happy Hours

Beer is plentiful and cheap in bars throughout Vietnam. You'll need to start early though, since most bars shut down between 10pm and midnight. A few are the exception, including Hair of the Dog Bar (open 'til 3 am) in *Ho Chi Minh City* and Temple Bar in *Hanoi*, which is open 24 hours a day.

While at most bars, it is quite cheap to have a drink, you can save even more money by heading to Happy Hours. Half price drinks, Buy 1, Get 1 free and free food with your beer are just a few of the offers you'll find during Happy Hour. Every bar offers a different schedule, so check first before you head out to drink.

If you want cheap traditional beer, look for bia hoi, a local fresh beer that is delivered daily in jugs. While it is only about 3% alcohol, bia hoi is considerably cheaper than other options and is ideal for social drinking. You'll find this beer in smaller bars and on street corners.

## Nightclubs Around Vietnam

Clubbing is a fun way to get out and about at night and Vietnam has no shortage of places to dance the night away. You'll certainly find more clubs in the bigger cities, but many smaller ones also have a club or two. *Nha Trang* and *Hoi An* both feature a few clubs that are quite popular with locals and tourists alike.

*Hanoi* offers the <u>Bar Déjà Vu</u> in the Sheraton Hotel, where a DJ plays until 1 am. The actual club does give you the boot at 2 am, though. The Dragonfly Club is another hotspot of activity, though crowded and definitely for a younger crowd.

If you're heading to *Ho Chi Minh City*, American Discotheque features two rooms with different music styles and is open until midnight. Gossip is a popular club for the who's who of the city, and Bounce Club is ideal for hip-hop lovers.

## Shisha

When you go to a modern bar, you can find <u>shisha</u> or hookah. These water pipes are quite popular around the country, though there is talk of banning shisha. For the time being, however, you can enjoy smoking fruity flavored tobacco through a water pipe in many bars and restaurants.

In Hanoi, head to the Old Quarter to find shisha bars or visit the Dragonfly Club's shisha room. Bazar in *Hoi An* is a good place to enjoy a multitude of shisha flavors, including traditional apple or something more exciting like banana or mint.

In *Ho Chi Minh City*, Vina Shisha is a good place to stop in for a smoke. You'll also find water pipes in most teashops around the city.

While *Ho Chi Minh City* may be the best place to enjoy the nightlife, *Hanoi* and *Hoi An* are also enjoyable cities for the night owls.

# Your Vietnam Bucket List

There is no denying that Vietnam is an amazing country. Now that you've learned about the culture and history of the area, it's time to look at the must-do activities at each destination.

We'll begin at the top of the country and work our way down. Each city lists the top activities that you just can't miss.

## Sapa

Sapa is a picturesque northern town that cannot be missed.

**1. Hike through Muong Hoa Valley.** This amazing day trip will take you along a river and through rice paddies and small towns.

**2. Swim in the Love Waterfall.** Just outside of *Sapa* is a beautiful waterfall where you can swim. Take the time to hike up the cliff to see the pagoda, too.

**3. People watch in Quang Truong Square.** The center of *Sapa* is a fascinating piece of local culture.

## Hanoi

The capital city of Vietnam is quieter than *Ho Chi Minh City*, but it is packed with things to see and do.

**1. Walk through the Old Quarter.** Enjoy shopping or eating in this warm section of the city. Don't forget to try the pho!

**2. Visit Mr. Ho Chi Minh.** The founder of modern Vietnam is on view under glass in his marble mausoleum.

**3. Tour Hoa Lo Prison.** See where American Prisoners during the war were kept and Vietnamese prisoners before that.

**4. Take in a water theater puppet show at Thang Long Theater.** This ancient art form is definitely a must-see.

**5. Shop at Dong Xuan Market.** Enjoy the sights and sounds of the best market in the city.

## Ha Long Bay

Just three hours from *Hanoi*, *Ha Long Bay* is a great day trip and there is plenty to do here.

**1. Rent a kayak and explore.** There are plenty of interesting sites to visit on the bay.

**2. Explore on bicycle.** The beautiful islands in the bay are ideal for cycling.

**3. Visit the floating villages.** Take a boat tour or kayak over to these floating shacks over freshwater pearl farms.

## Hue

Hue was once the capital of Vietnam and is home to a number of historical sites.

**1. See the royal tombs.** There are plenty of tombs around Hue in varying conditions, all of which are interesting to check out.

**2. Check out the tiger-fighting arena.** Ho Quyen was once used to host fights between elephants and tigers. Today it is inactive, but fascinating.

**3. Soak in the hot springs at Thanh Tan.** This water park includes both hot and cold springs, as well as a wave pool.

## Hoi An

*Hoi An* is a pleasant little town that is friendly and interesting.

**1. Listen to live music.** There is live music to be found every night of the week in this town, so check it out.

**2. Sleep by the rice paddies.** A homestay overlooking rice paddies is an experience you will never forget.

**3. Celebrate the full moon.** On the 14th day of each lunar month, there is a full moon party in *Hoi An*. It's an exhilarating experience that you can't miss.

## Nha Trang

This coastal city is the perfect place to visit when you want a little rest and relaxation.

**1. Chill on the beach.** *Nha Trang* is well known for its beautiful beaches, so take advantage. Go snorkeling while you're there.

**2. Learn to cook traditional meals.** Take a cooking class with a friend or on your own to learn local dishes.

**3. Cruise the islands.** Take a boat tour to get a close up look at the 71 islands just off the coast of *Nha Trang*.

## Mui Ne

Tucked away near *Phan Thiet*, this town is a relaxing place to stay for a few days.

**1. Take a quad to the dunes.** Enjoy riding an quad over the sand and stop to watch the sun set over the sea.

**2. Visit the Red Dunes.** These unique sand dunes are not that far from the white dunes where sand boarding is popular.

**3. Walk the Fairy Stream.** Not far from *Mui Ne,* this stream winds through green trees and limestone formations and ends in a waterfall.

## Phan Thiet

*Phan Thiet* is a popular tourist destination, but don't let this deter you from visiting.

**1. Go kite surfing.** You haven't lived until you've been pulled through the water on a board by a giant kite!

**2. Visit Po Sah Inu Cham Tower.** This 7th century tower is worth checking out, along with the other ruins in the area.

**3. Stuff yourself with fresh seafood.** You can even pick the food you want while it's still alive and watch it being cooked.

## Ho Chi Minh City

This bustling city is a destination for nearly everyone passing through Vietnam and has a lot to offer.

**1. Crawl through the Cu Chi Tunnels.** See where Vietnamese soldiers hid from the enemy.

**2. Negotiate prices in Ben Thanh Market.** This is the best market in the city and well worth a visit.

**3. Enjoy banh xeo on on Dinh Công Tráng street.** Taste a few different variations of this local dish.

**4. Cruise the Saigon River.** Take a dinner cruise and enjoy the sights as you eat delicious food.

**5. Tour the museums.** *Ho Chi Minh City* is packed with museums that cover every period of history. Make a day trip or two of it.

There is plenty more to explore in these towns, as well as others in Vietnam, but this bucket list will get you off to a good start. You really don't want to miss anything on this list.

# The Ultimate Laos Travel Guide

## Discover the Lao Cuisine and Discover the Lao Nature

# Map of Laos

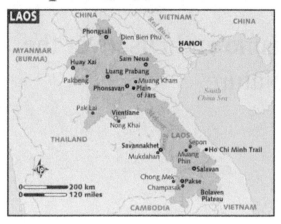

# Does Laos Intrigue You?

The very fact that you are reading this means you're interested in traveling to Laos. This amazing country may be small, but it is packed with culture and friendly people. The country has a turbulent past that has helped develop the uniqueness that is Laos.

Laos has been controlled by the French, manhandled by China and North Vietnam and has had its own share of internal conflicts. In fact, the country has only known peace for the past two decades, so it's an interesting place to visit. The tourism industry is just starting to take off, but it is still relatively untouched.

If you're looking for a pristine part of the world to visit, where only a few tourists have trekked, Laos is the ideal place to go. With 21% of the country dedicated to habitat conservation, there are plenty of places to explore and the cultural sites are even more amazing.

Here, you will find stunning Buddhist temples, colonial buildings, ancient temples and astoundingly beautiful natural sites. In fact, in 2013, Laos won the "World's Best Tourist Destination" thanks to its culture and history.

Get ready to experience a truly unique place in the world. Laos is unlike any other country, thanks to the unique blend of cultures found here. You'll find it is just as amazing as you imagine it to be.

Now let's get started!

# Where to Stay While Travelling Laos

Finding a place to sleep each night is usually the principle preoccupation for a traveler planning his or her journey. With tourism on the rise in Laos, you'll find a wide range of options to choose from.

One of the things I highly recommend to all travelers is staying in a homestay at least once. This is such a great opportunity to create memories with a local family and it provides an experience that you just won't get anywhere else.

Living with a local family will allow you to experience the culture in a unique way. You'll eat traditional foods and live in a traditional way. Unless you are staying with a wealthier family, expect squat toilets in the houses, a true local living experience! Oftentimes, the family will invite you to participate in activities in the village with them, too.

Finding a homestay can be a little tricky. You'll probably want to plan for a hotel or hostel the first few nights, since you'll need to arrange most homestays once you get there. Local language schools and travel agencies can guide you to the right place. However, you can also ask around in any village you visit. A night's stay will run you around $5-10, depending on the quality of the home.

Of course, for those who prefer more independence, a hotel may be a better option. Depending on quality, you can pay anything from $20 to $100 a night, though smaller towns have even lower prices.

Try checking out Booking.com to pre-book your hotel. You can also simply find one once you arrive. Asking people on the street is a good way to find cheaper accommodation, though it may not be for everyone. If you feel the need to plan everything out ahead of time, you'll probably want to book your place to stay early on.

Other options for accommodation range from hostels to vacation home rentals. Hostels are a fun way to get to know your fellow travelers and maybe even find someone to travel with. They usually have shared dorm rooms for a fraction of the price that hotels charge, plus you'll have access to a kitchen and other amenities. While everything is shared, there's no better way to bond with others than to cook and eat meals together.

In Vientiane, you'll have a choice of several options, including the Ventiane Backpacker's Hostel, which is clean and well rated, or the Funky Monkey Hostel, known for its fun atmosphere. If you're staying in Luang Prabang, look for the Kounsavan Guest House or Khammany Inn Hostel, both of which are comfortable and clean, with a good reputation. Check HostelWorld.com to find even more options.

Prices for hostels range from $5-10 a night for low end places and may be slightly above this for higher quality. As long as you don't mind sharing spaces, you'll find that hostels are quite accommodating.

Vacation rentals are another good option, particularly if you plan to stay in an area for a while or if you are traveling in a larger group. Rather than rent several hotel rooms for everyone, you can just rent a house. This is also a great choice for traveling families. AirBnB is one of the best places to find available homes and apartments. You'll have a home away from home with this method.

In addition to being able to cook for your family, having the space to move around and go to sleep without other disturbing your slumber can be a very nice perk. Renting a home doesn't have to be expensive either, you can spend anywhere from $15 for a private room to $30+ for a whole place of your own.

Wherever you choose to stay while you are in Laos, you'll spend little time in your accommodation, since there is so much to see and do around the country.

# Moving Around in Laos

Most small towns in Laos are easy enough to walk around. You will only find transport necessary when you are in a larger city, though options are limited. Vientiane, for example, is the only place you'll find city buses. In most cases, you'll find that buses are a waste of time, however.

## In-City Travel

While you are trying to get around Vientiane or a similar city, your options are somewhat limited. Taxis exist, but are generally used by foreign business people. You can expect to pay just under $50 to hire a taxi to take you around for the day. Make sure you negotiate your trip before you get into the taxi, as meters are non-existent.

Tuk tuks are found around most towns and are a good way to get where you need to go. They are also referred to as jumbos or saam-laaw. Essentially, they are a three wheeled cart pulled by a motorcycle engine. Negotiate your price before getting in.

Motorcycles can also be rented and you can head out on the open road, if you so desire. Just be sure to take along a driver's license and your helmet. If you are stopped, it's helpful to have the necessary papers on you. While technically, you can rent a bike without any formalities, it's best to avoid problems.

## Long Distance Travel

If you're planning to travel between towns, you'll need a good way to do so. Buses are fairly common and popular, but will likely drop you off at least a kilometer out of town. This can be frustrating if you have luggage, so plan to walk or find a taxi to take you into town.

As in many Asian countries, pickups are a common method of transport. The backs are converted into seating areas with benches lining either side to allow for maximum capacity.

If you're in a hurry, there is a surprisingly impressive aviation industry within the country. Fly in and out of the main cities to save time, though not money.

Rivers are so plentiful in Laos, that it's not surprising there are plenty of boats. The country may be landlocked, but it has no shortage of boats. Head to the nearest river and find out if anyone is going in your direction, or take a river taxi or ferry. The most popular trip is taking the ferry from Huay Xai to Luang Prabang. You'll pay around $25 for a two-day trip and it allows you to see everything on the river. However, be aware that there are no cabins and you will be sleeping and traveling on the outside decks.

River taxis are much faster and can get you where you want to go. They are best for short trips, though, and they charge by the hour usually. Boat types include:

**Speedboats:** This is the quickest way to get around the river communities, but it's also the most dangerous.

**Longtail Boat:** These are the boats that you'll find just about anywhere in the country. They are simple in design, with a rotating engine at the back. They will get you where you need to go pretty quickly.

**Rowboat:** Designed as a basic dugout canoe, these rowboats are fine for crossing smaller rivers, but they're too slow to really make them useful for transport otherwise.

**Double Deck Boats:** These are rare nowadays, but they can still be found. They're referred to as heua sah and are very slow.

Another option for getting around is to rent a car. You can drive yourself, but it's usually just more convenient and fairly affordable to get a car with a driver. Avoid getting lost and many other issues this way.

# Eating in Laos: A Culinary Adventure

Food in Laos is a little different than the food you'll find in the surrounding countries. Nearly everything is made with fresh ingredients and you will find that this results in incredibly mouthwatering dishes. Cooks here are also quite aware of herbs and use them extensively. You will definitely want to try the local cuisine.

With a heavy French influence, you'll find that many restaurants in Laos actually serve French food. Others have adapted to provide a blend of cuisines, including Thai and Vietnamese, which can be pretty interesting. While restaurants are a good way to spend your early days, don't forget to test out the street food, too. It's not to be missed.

Food in Laos tends to be flavored with plenty of spice and the hotter, the better. Be aware of this, since you can burn your taste buds if you're not careful. Taste your dish before adding anything extra like garlic or chili, since it may already be hot enough.

## A Sticky Rice Primer

One constant in Lao cuisine is sticky rice. It is served with nearly everything and every meal will have a basket or bowl of it. Sticky rice is the national staple food of Laos and you should have an idea how to eat it before you arrive.

This rice is short grain rice that is particularly glutinous. When cooked, it forms a starch that helps bind the rice together. It can be tricky to eat if you're trying to use chopsticks or a spoon, so the traditional method is the best way to go.

To eat sticky rice "properly" you need to use your hands. Take a small amount of rice and squeeze it slightly to make a ball. You can then use it to dip in sauces and eat. However, the dish is also used as an implement, much like tortillas in Mexico. Use your fingers to lightly shape the rice ball into a scoop and you can use it to spoon food to your mouth. Watch how the locals do it and you'll catch on quickly.

Here's a quick video to show you how to eat sticky rice, if you're still wondering what to do.

## Dining Out at Restaurants and Cafes

When you just want to sit down and rest for a bit, try settling in at a café and ordering an iced coffee. This is a tall glass of coffee with condensed milk added, a sweet and chilly beverage that will help you beat the Laos heat and give you a boost in energy.

Of course, there are plenty of other foods available in the eateries that are spread around the cities. It's worth trying at least one French restaurant while you are in Vientiane. Though pricier than other places, you'll experience authentic French food at a fraction of the price you would pay in Paris. L'Adresse de Tinay is considered to be one of the best for this type of food and is surprisingly affordable. If nothing else, stop in for some of their exquisite desserts.

Apart from the delicacies that French cuisine has to offer, Laos restaurants provide a nice range of tasty dishes that you can enjoy for just a few dollars. Appetizers are plenty and usually consist of pork or beef, made into sausages, meatballs or simply dried. You'll also find pickled pork rinds and fish are popular.

Kaipen is made of fried algae and is often served with a meal in restaurants or well you're waiting. You may also find khau pak bong, or stir-fried water spinach and fried moss, Mekong River Moss, on the menu.

When it comes to ordering a salad in a restaurant, watch for the names to tell you what they might contain. Sarad is usually a vegetarian affair with an assortment of vegetables and herbs. However, laap or larb is a salad that includes meat, often with fish sauce mixed in.

Nem Neung is something every traveler should try. This fresh dish includes rice noodles, pork sausage and fresh salad greens, green banana and star fruit. If you sit down to eat the dish in a restaurant, you'll be served each component separately, along with rice paper to wrap it all up in. There is a delightful sauce that is served with the mixture.

Soups are a big thing here and there are entire restaurants that specialize in just one kind of soup. Pork noodle soup is particularly popular and has many variations throughout the cities, but most of them are pretty good. The thin broth is the base of this soup, to which a large number of ingredients are added, including chili, fish sauce, lime, noodles, pork strips, vinegar, galangal and others. Every bowl of soup you try will taste somewhat different and you can add your own extras to the basic soup.

Other soups include Kaeng galee, or Lao curry, tom padaek, which is spicy fish cooked in a padaek base, and or, a green stew made with vegetables. In Luang Prabang, ask for or lam, a specialty green stew made in that town only.

Meat is often included in the main meal and it may be steamed or grilled. Sometimes, meats are fried, but this is more often found in the street stalls. Steaming is a popular option and most meat will be tucked into a banana leaf before being steamed. The leaf helps seal in the moisture and also imparts a pleasant flavor. Try titi gai (steamed steak), mok gai (steamed chicken) or mok pa (steamed fish).

Grilled meat is even more commonly found and the charcoal and open flames add plenty of flavor to the dishes prepared this way. You can get quite a few different meats that have been marinated in a mixture that is usually specific to the restaurant. Ping gai refers to grilled chicken that was previously marinated, while ping ped is duch, ping seen is beef and ping moo is pork.

Feeling adventurous and have a strong stomach? Then you might want to try ordering chicken feet that have been marinated and then roasted. Ping theen gai may not look appetizing, but it's surprisingly good.

Seen dat is a great meal to enjoy at a restaurant. This is essentially barbecue done Laos-style. A large dome is set over a fire and assorted meats and vegetables are cooked over it. You choose what you want to eat and it will be cooked up for you, on the spot.

Dessert is a good way to end a meal anywhere and Laos is no different. Sticky rice is often the base of a delicious sweet. You'll find it mixed with coconut and mango in khao niao mak muang and topped with red beans, coconut milk, sugar and coconut in khao lam.

Khao tom are delicious steamed rice balls that are stuffed with taro or bananas most frequently and cooked in a banana leaf. Khao pard is a layered jelly cake made of rice and pandan leaves, while voon is a jelly made from coconut milk. You'll also want to try sangkaya, a tasty custard made with squash that no one can resist for long.

## Street Food in Laos

Eating on the street can result in an upset tummy if you're not careful, but the risk is worth it, in my opinion. As long as you take care, you'll find that this is the cheapest, most delicious way to taste test the local foods. I always recommend that people try street food at least once in their stay in a foreign country.

If you find yourself in Vientiane, head to the Vientiane Dalat Pi, a delightful market that is full of street food. You'll find just about every type of Lao food here and if you go fairly early, you'll find it all freshly made. In Luang Prabang, you'll want to check out the Phosi Market.

Throughout the country, you'll find baguettes, a remnant of the French occupation. Called khao jee, these long breads are sold with a variety of fillings. These include pate made from pork liver or boiled pork sausage. The toppings are almost always carrot and radish salad, along with cucumber and the condiments generally include mayonnaise with hot sauce. These simple sandwiches are tasty and quite filling.

Laab moo or minced pork salad is another popular dish that you will find both on the street and in small shops and restaurants. This is a delicious blend of minced pork, coriander, mint, chili and shallots, with lime and fish sauce mixed in. Make sure the laab you buy is cooked . . .there's also a raw version which is almost guaranteed to cause stomach problems. Laab moo is usually served with the staple sticky rice.

Other salads abound in the street stalls. One that is fairly notable is tam mak hoong, which is quite similar to Thailand's som tam. This delightful salad is made with green papaya, lime, chili, and tomatoes, along with other ingredients. The result is a very spicy salad that resembles a noodle dish. Depending on the region, you'll find it served with makok (a sour fruit), crab or pickled fish.

If you want something a little more substantial, spring rolls are a good choice. They are similar to those made in Vietnam, rice paper is wrapped around rice noodles and plenty of fresh green vegetables, along with shrimp, pork or another meat. Most stalls will offer at least one or two sauces to dip your rolls in. You can also find fried versions of this popular delicacy.

For travelers who prefer more meat in their meals, there are plenty of street stalls to oblige. Lao beef jerky or sien savanh, is a handy snack that is marinated and dried, then grilled and served. It's a chewy snack that is usually served with some sticky rice. You might prefer to opt for sausages, however. Laos street stalls offer sai oua, which is a rather spicy combination of ground pork with kaffir lime, lemongrass and a number of

hotter spices to give it some real kick. Again, this is usually served with sticky rice.

Skewers are also plentiful, particularly in the night markets. You will find everything from an entire fish roasted on a skewer to chicken breasts and snakes. Even pork ribs are sold on a stick. These are usually rubbed down with lemongrass before being roasted over an open fire. The taste is unique and definitely something worth trying.

Noodles and sticky rice tend to be the base of many dishes and just about everything that has meat in it will come with a side of sticky rice. However, noodles tend to stand on their own and can be found with a variety of sauces, chilies and chopped vegetables and herbs. These are usually sold in banana leaf packets and make a terrific snack late at night.

Once you've filled up on fish, pork and noodles, it's time for dessert. Lao desserts are some of the best I've found in my travels and you'll probably find that you eat entirely too many of them. It's hard to resist coconut cakes, carefully fried in a cast iron mold until crispy on the outside. The insides are still gooey and the whole thing is served in a banana leaf.

Crepes can also be found at many street carts. While some are the delicate French kind of crepe, many are thicker and almost pancake. These tasty concoctions are fried for extra flavor and then smothered in sweet milk. You can find them with a number of different toppings, though the traditional kind comes with bananas and eggs.

Lod xong is an interesting looking dessert that is much tastier than it looks. Lod xong is green and is made up of palm sugar, rice jelly and coconut milk. You'll also find plenty of nam van sold at different stands. There is no one recipe for this sweet dish, but it usually includes a few tropical fruits and tapioca.

If you're still leary of eating in the street, you have another option available to you. You can head to the market and make your own food at your hostel or vacation rental.

## Buying in the Market

You'll find that buying your own food in the market is the best way to go if you have access to a kitchen. There are plenty of tasty fruits and vegetables there that you'll recognize . . . as well as a few that you may not.

While you're in the market, plan to try some new things. There's nothing wrong with eating what you're used to and that may be the reason you are shopping for your own ingredients, but it would be a shame if you didn't try:

Dragonfruit: This scaly fruit looks very alien with its bright pink skin. Inside, you'll find white flesh with small black seeds. Some varieties come with a purple flesh. Both types have a mild taste and are vaguely reminiscent of kiwi.

**Durian:** The stinkiest fruit in the world is also one of the best tasting, according to nearly everyone who has tried it. While the spiky looking fruit smells pretty awful, the custardy yellow insides are sheer heaven.

**Rambutan:** Bright red fruit with long hairs sticking out, rambutan looks almost as alien as dragonfruit. The delicate interior tastes like lychee and is sweet and tender with a large pit. You'll find yourself gobbling these up if you buy a bag of them.

**Mangosteen:** Big and round, the purple mangosteen fruit is peeled to reveal thick, white pieces of fruit that taste similar to lychee. They are very good and quite addictive with the sweet, almost crisp flesh.

**Rose Apple:** The little pink or red fruits are crunchy and watery. While they tend to be a little sweet, they can also be somewhat tart. The center is hollow, so this is an easy fruit to eat.

Of course, there is more than fruit to be found in the market, so don't be afraid to check out the vegetables, too.

If you're feeling particularly adventurous, you can find a wide range of grilled insects, including bee larvae, worms, crickets and others. There are also bats, rodents and snakes for sale, often completely whole, though you can request that the vendor skin and gut them. Blood, usually from cows, is also sold in congealed cubes to add to soups and other dishes.

The market is quite the adventure on its own, but there's plenty more to see!

# What You Should See in Laos

Laos is a pretty fascinating country. Since it is only just starting to ramp up the tourism, there are plenty of places to visit with minimal other people. In some cases, you'll be completely by yourself.

## Temples and Historical Sites

Laos has quite the long history and this is evident everywhere you go. You'll see an odd mix of French architecture and native designs, but most travelers are looking for temples, of which there are many.

You needn't venture out of the capital city far to find everything you want in a temple. Wat Si Saket is right inside the city and has a long cloister wall that is full of miniature Buddhas from the 16$^{th}$ and 19$^{th}$ centuries. There are nearly 7,000 of the figures, elaborated in metal, stone and wood.

Also in Vientiane is Pha That Luang, a gorgeous golden temple that is rumored to have held a bone from Buddha's body. While this may be just legend, the stupa is worth checking out. Take a look at That Dam, too. It was once covered in gold, but thieves stole it all and now the place is known as the Black Stupa and is said to have a 7 headed naga inside.

Another popular tourist spot is Wat Si Muang, which is a Buddhist temple in the capital. It was built in the 16$^{th}$ century and has a rather unique look to it. The current building was built on top of the ruins of a Khmer shrine and there are still pieces of this visible in the area.

If you head south, you'll find Wat Phu in the province of Champasak to be quite interesting. This ruined temple dates back to before Angkor Wat was originally built. You can still make out the detail in many areas of the temple and views from the hill are incredible. There's a spring nearby which is said to produce holy water.

When it comes to historical sites, you can't miss the Plain of Jars. This is a unique area that surrounds Phonsavan. It is full of granite and sandstone jars that were carved from the rock over 2,000 years ago. No one knows exactly what they were used for. Legends range from urns for dead bodies to jars to store wine. It's certainly an interesting view and you can decide for yourself what these mysterious jars once held.

Of course, not all historic sights are as ancient. In 1969, the US sent cement to Laos to build an airport. Instead of using it for this purpose, the locals built a replica of the Arc de Triomphe, which they called the Victory Monument. To expats, it's known as the vertical runway. You can climb the tower to see the entire city.

## Museums and Other Interesting Sights

For those who love to learn more about a country's history, the Lao National Museum is a good place to start. It's based in Vientiane, in a French colonial building that once housed the Governor. The ground floor has ancient historical artifacts, including pottery, stone jars and dinosaur bones, among other things. On the second floor, you'll find more information on the modern history of the country, including the French inhabitation and the Vietnam War, when the US military was a strong presence in the area.

The capital city is also home to the fascinating Buddha Park, which has been around for decades, but is still a relatively young site. The park is not just dedicated to Buddha, despite the name. You'll find Hindu gods here, as well. This is due to the fact that the monk who built the park was studying both religions at the time. You can eat and drink coffee in the park's café once you have finished wandering around the statues.

If you are in Pakse, check out the Champasak Provincial Museum for some interesting information. This museum focuses exclusively on this area of the country. You'll find everything from a 12$^{th}$ century water jar and jewelry to musical instruments and fabric. Though relatively small, the museum is packed with information for the interested visitor.

## Explore the Natural Side of Laos

This country has so much beauty that it would be a shame to miss out on it. Head to Nam Ha near Luang Namtha to visit the Biodiversity Park there. This protected area is a lovely spot to simply wander around and take photos. You might even get lucky and see a leopard. There are also elephants living here and a wide variety of plants.

A short trip by boat from Pakse you will find The Four Thousand Islands. These are small islands that dot the Mekong River. For those interested in just relaxing, this is a good spot to enjoy. It's very quiet and most people end up just walking around or renting a bicycle to enjoy the scenery.

Also in this area is Bolaven Plateau, a historically important area of the country. Despite being a major part of the Vietnam War, the plateau is now home to coffee plantations, hiking trails and numerous waterfalls to explore. You may also want to check out the markets here, since they offer goods that are not available elsewhere in Laos. If you do visit, don't leave the marked paths, as there are still a large number of UXO around (unexploded ordnance).

In the tiny province of Bokeo, there is a wonderful trek that you can take to a zip line. The Gibbon Experience is similar to zip lines in other countries, but here you will find a black crested gibbon species that was once considered extinct. The journey is usually a three-day trip, well worth the nights spent in the jungle.

Getting tired of sightseeing? It might be time to settle down for a drink.

# Exciting Things to Do

Laos may not have any seaside beaches, but it does just fine without them. No traveler will ever be bored in this particular country. There's so much to see and do that you'll find yourself having to narrow down your list and deciding on the biggest priorities.

## Water Sports

Since Laos is a landlocked country, you can't find things like kitesurfing and diving here, but there plenty of rivers to enjoy. Tubing is a great way to take in the sights along the river. While it may be fairly tranquil most of the time, rapids can give you quite the rush.

While Laos was once known for its tubing parties, where people would stop every so often along the river to drink, that practice is now prohibited. Too many people were injured or even killed during these events. Today, tubing is back to the way it should be, a sightseeing tour that is alcohol-free.

Head to Vang Vieng if you want to go tubing down the Nam Song River. You'll be able to rent an inner tube or a kayak and take off down the river. It's a great way to check out the scenery.

## Climbing and Spelunking

Laos is a country full of beautiful mountains. While this makes getting around a challenge and everything takes longer than it should, it also means that there are some amazing cliff climbs.

For rock climbing, Vang Vieng is the best known area to visit. There are several areas to climb, including the Sleeping Wall with 14 different climbing routes, near the Nam Song River. The Sleeping Cave is nearby and offers just nine climbing paths, but if you're willing to travel a little further, you can visit Tham Nam Them (15 routes) or Pha Daeng Mountain, which has eight different paths to climb. Both of these feature small caves, as well as some fun climbing.

Avoid climbing the slippery cliffs during the rainy season, as it can be considerably more dangerous at this time of year. The rainy season starts in July and runs through October.

Mountains also feature caves, which the more adventurous may want to explore. Konglor Cave is definitely a must-see attraction. It's not easy to get to, so going through a travel agency is probably your best bet. If you are feeling particularly adventurous, it takes nearly a day to go by public transport from Vientiane to Ban Hua Hin.

There are small villages on either side of the 7.5 km cave, where you can find homestays. You'll need to hire a boat to get through the cave, as it is full of water, but there are areas where the water is not deep enough and walking is necessary. Bring water shoes for these sections and a headlamp so you can see the amazing interior of the cave.

The Pak Ou Caves or Buddha Caves near Ban Pak Ou, are also worth a trip. You'll probably want to take a boat down the Mekong, though it's possible to get there by land, too. The river is definitely the more scenic of the two methods. The caves themselves are not large, but they are full of images and statues of Buddha, which makes them a fun side trip.

Other caving options include the Xe Bang Fai cave, Muang Noi caves and even more small caving expeditions around Vang Vieng.

## Exploring

Ready to have some real fun? Head out and do some exploring on your own! Just be careful to stick to the trails since there are still unexploded mines and bombs in some areas and you really don't want to trip over them. If there's a trail, however, you should be safe.

Cycling is a good way to get some exercise and see the area, but keep in mind that Laos is very mountainous and you are going to be getting a serious workout. Perhaps a better option would be taking a motorbike instead. In Vang Vieng, you can rent a bicycle or a motorbike and explore the area yourself or with a guide.

There are plenty of motorcycle tours you can take, as well. One of these is MotoLao, which offers tours around the country, both on-road and off. They also provide 4x4 tours if you want to really get off the beaten path. You can also try Laos Adventure Riders Association, based out of Vientiane. They offer bike rentals and tours.

Another fun way to see the sights in Vang Vieng is to take a hot air balloon ride. The view is stunning and the experience is one of a kind. It's not cheap, but the memories will stick with you forever.

Heading into nature isn't for everyone, but Laos is also a place where you can enjoy hanging out with friends and drinking beer.

# Laos Nightlife: What to Expect

If it's partying you're after, Laos is not your best option. The country is fairly laid back and many restaurants offer nothing more than the local beer. There are no real nightclubs here, though some bars are livelier than others, so you may want to head to Thailand if you're only traveling for the party.

That being said, nightlife is not dead in Laos. You just need to know where to go. Most of the larger cities have a wide range of bars, including expat bars, to check out.

## Drinking Locally

While in Laos, you will definitely have to sample some of the local drinks. One of the most commonly found alcohols is lao-lao, a rather strong moonshine that is made from sticky rice hulls. This drink is pretty strong, around 40% proof. You'll find it offered in many small towns and rural areas where the locals enjoy giving tourists free drinks just to see the reaction.

Lao-lao is generally plain, but it can be found with insects, snakes and other reptiles added to it for extra kick. This is definitely not for the weak of stomach.

For the less adventurous, Beer Lao is a popular brand of beer found throughout the country. You can get it anywhere that sells beer. Though rather bland, the beer is pretty cheap. You can also find Beer Lao Gold or Black, which have slightly different flavors.

## Where to Party

Most areas of Laos are fairly quiet, but the larger cities have a little nightlife if you know where to look. Even the bigger cities are somewhat subdued, but there are still bars to hang out at.

When in Vientiane, you have a number of options. One popular place to visit is Spirit House. While this pleasant bar and restaurant isn't open that late (only until 11 pm), it's a good place to start off in an elegant atmosphere. Another very well known place is Bor Pen Nyang, which is THE place to go if you are a backpacker. It's also a popular hangout for expats and locals, so it's a good place to meet up with some interesting people.

If drinking is what you're after, head to the Belgian Beer Bar, where you can sample a wide range of imported and local beers. There's plenty of tasty food to order here, as well and the ambiance is a fun, relaxed one.

Luang Prabang is another common destination for travelers and it has a few bars of its own to offer. The 1861 Bar is a very sophisticated, elegant place, with a French colonial theme. Here you'll enjoy liquors and assorted drinks from around the world. For more of a nightclub vibe, you'll want to head to Dao Fa, which is just outside of town. It's a hopping place to visit and definitely the nightclub scene in this area of the country.

It may seem like there isn't a lot to the Laos nightlife scene, but if you really do want to party it up, then you'll need to visit Vang Vieng. Here, there are plenty of places to drink. Enjoy Oh La La with its infamous mojitos and typical décor, or the local Irish Pub. This town is known for its "happy shakes" or mushroom milkshakes that are rumored to leave you out of it for up to three days.

Most bars and restaurants close by midnight throughout the country, so you'll be refreshed and ready for action the next morning. Unless, of course, there was a party in your hostel overnight.

# Your Laos Bucket List

## Luang Prabang

This pleasant town is a World Heritage City and has more than enough sights to keep you interested. The French colonial architecture is just the beginning.

**1. Visit the night market.** This market is open from 5-9:30 every evening and is a good place to find gifts if you are willing to bargain.

**2. Trek up Mount Phousi.** The incredible views are worth the 300 stair steps to the top of the mountain. Here you will also find Wat Chomsi.

**3. Check out the Bear Rescue Center.** Located near the Kuang Sii Waterfalls, the Bear Rescue Center keeps bears safe from bile farms that harvest their bile.

## Vang Vieng

Known as being a party town, Vang Vieng is actually a great place to enjoy nature. The town is near several climbing spots, as well as a couple of rivers.

**1. Go tubing on Nam Song.** This is the thing to do if you are spending more than a couple of hours in Vang Vieng, so go for it.

**2. Explore a cave or two.** This part of Laos is full of caves, both big and small. If you're into spelunking, check them out.

**3. Try a whiskey bucket.** This unique blend of cola, whiskey, Red Bull, lime, honey and ice is unique to this particular town.

**4. Try the street food.** Street stalls abound here and offer a wide range of delicious snacks to try out.

**5. Relax and watch local fishermen cast their nets.** The soothing rhythm of net casting is fun to watch when you are in the mood to relax. Head to the riverbank to find some fishermen.

# Vientiane

The capital of Laos is surprisingly tranquil and relaxing. You'll enjoy your visit here, as it is packed with local culture and plenty of history.

**1. Shop in the night market.** A night market is the best place to get deals on souvenirs and sample the street food.

**2. Detox with a herbal sauna or papaya body scrub.** At the Papaya Spa, you can enjoy some relaxation time and get rid of the aches and pains that come with exploring the country.

**3. Visit That Luang.** This impressive stupa is one of the most sacred in Laos and is so beautiful you really need to check it out.

**4. Stroll through Buddha Park.** The many statues in this pristine park include Hindu gods, as well as multiple images of Buddha.

**5. Explore the Lao National Museum.** You'll find out all about the history of Laos here and it is well worth a visit.

# Muang Khammouan

While Muang Khammouan may be a small town, it is the destination for anyone interested in checking out Kong Lor Cave. The area around the town is breathtaking and worth a visit.

**1. Take a look at Kong Lor Cave.** This 7.5 km cave requires a boat to get through, but it's an amazing trip.

**2. Visit the Buddha Cave.** Check out thousands of images of Buddha crammed into two small caves.

**3. Explore Pha That Sikhottabong.** This beautiful religious site is best known for its very tall stupa and the seated Buddha that adorns it.

# Savannakhet

Located on the Mekong River, Savannakhet is a popular spot for those who are leaving Thailand for a visa run. Here, you'll find quiet streets and rowdy expats alike. There are things to see and do, but it's a good spot to just relax.

## 1. Watch the monks make their morning route around town.
You'll have to get up early to catch a glimpse of the monks walking their route as people give them food.

## 2. Gamble a little at the Savan Vegas Casino.
Lots of expats enjoy hanging out here and it's a fun place to spend a little time. Just don't throw away all your money!

## 3. Dine at the Daosavanh Restaurant.
This French restaurant is just the place to entertain your palate while you're in town.

## Pakse

Travelers often overlook this quiet city, but it is worth checking out. In the southern part of Laos, you'll find quite a few things to see and do.

## 1. Check out Tadfane Waterfalls.
Just outside of Pakse, this impressive waterfall is worth a visit.

## 2. Visit the Champasak Historic Museum.
Do you enjoy art? Then this museum should be on your list of places to see. It includes a number of Khmer artifacts and local art.

## 3. Visit the Luang Temple.
This ancient temple is stunning from the outside, but inside you'll find some amazing relics from Laos's history.

# The Ultimate Cambodia Travel Guide

## Discover The Temples Of Angkor

# Map Of Cambodia

# Ready Up For Cambodia

You hold in your hands a guide to one of the most fascinating countries in Asia. Cambodia is a place packed with history and culture and it is impossible to visit it without being changed at least a little.

Since you've picked this book up, I can only assume that you're considering a trip to this amazing place. You won't be sorry if you do.

This is one of the countries in the area with a very difficult history. With the many cultural influences over the generations and the not-so-distant genocide that was committed by the Khmer Rouge, Cambodia is a country that is still coming into its own. It's the perfect time to visit, since tourism is just starting to pick up and there are still plenty of sights to see that don't charge an arm and a leg just because you're foreign.

The entire country is steeped in history and full of amazing sights that everyone can enjoy. From museums to ancient temples, there's plenty to see, but you don't have to spend all your time in the past. Visit Siem Reap to meet amazing, friendly people and to really participate in the culture. Phnom Penh is another popular place to hang out and it definitely feels more modern than some of the rural areas.

Cambodia features a wide range of cuisine, from China and Thailand to Vietnam and French. There's a little of everything mixed into the food here, which makes it particularly interesting to try a little bit of all the dishes. You'll find everything from noodle soup and salted baby clams to iced coffee and ice cream sandwiches available in the streets, as well as more sophisticated meals in the local restaurants.

You don't need a lot of money to enjoy traveling in Cambodia. It's a very affordable place to find adventure and while some touristy sites are more expensive, the place is cheap overall.

If you're looking for the adventure of a lifetime, why not explore this barely touched nation?

# Where To Stay In The Country Of Temples

Cambodia has plenty to offer when it comes to accommodation. You'll find five star hotels here that feel like you are in any Western country, but the real gems are the hotels and hostels that are hidden away and not as noticeable.

Booking.com is an excellent place to find a hotel in Siem Reap or any of the other large cities in Cambodia. Hotels can range from $30-100 a night, costing more if you stick to the top ones.

Whether you are traveling in the city or in more rural areas, there's something for every taste. Save some money and help the country's economy by choosing smaller, privately owned guesthouses and inns. These are the places that will have the most culture, but they also offer the best prices in many cases.

In Siem Reap, try the Popular Guesthouse, which is aptly named. Not only is it cheap to stay here, but the accommodations are very comfortable and pleasant. In Phnom Penh, The Laughing Fat Man is a good option, or you might want to try Aqua Boutique Guesthouse, which is just as charming as it sounds.

AirBnB is a good place to find guesthouses and rental homes if you prefer to stay on your own and want the comfort of a house. There are vacation rentals available that may be a better option than a hotel, particularly if you are traveling in a group.

I always recommend homestays for those who are interested in really getting a feel for a country and its culture. Cambodia is no exception. This beautiful country is inhabited by wonderful people and it would be a shame to travel through Cambodia without making some local friends.

Of course, you can always make friends outside of the accommodation, but this is the best possible way to experience the Khmer lifestyle.

Another low cost option is to stay in a hostel. There are plenty of them scattered around the country and they start at around $5 a night, per person. This will get you a dorm room and plenty of fun roomies, but there are private rooms available in many hostels, too.

These accommodations usually provide a kitchen where you can prepare your own food and a common room to hang out with other travelers. The atmosphere is a pleasant one and you're bound to meet plenty of interesting people.

You can book a hostel before you arrive (through Hostels.com or HostelWorld.com), or play it by ear once you arrive. In Siem Reap, try Siem Reap Rooms Guesthouse or Lotus Lodge, which offers a pool for its guests. In Phnom Penh, Hostel Nomads is centrally located and nice and clean, while Here Be Dragons is one of the best choices in Battambang.

# Getting From Here to There

Making your way around Cambodia is half the fun of visiting the country. The methods of transportation here are rustic for the most part, but it can be a lesson in learning to go with the flow.

## Local Transportation Options

Trying to make your way from one end of the city to the other? When you are attempting to move around the more urban areas, you have a few options, all of which have their quirks. It's a lot of fun to try all of the different methods of getting around.

Tuk tuks, or motorcycles with a little cabin on the back to carry a couple of passengers, are one of the touristic methods of traveling in small groups in some of the larger cities. Locals tend not to use tuk tuks, preferring the moto-remorque, which is similar to the tuk tuk in that it is powered by a motorbike, but has a longer carriage that can hold quite a few people. The moto-remorques are basically mini buses and are most used by locals.

In cities and large towns, you'll see motodops, which are usually just motorbikes that allow you to ride behind the driver for a low price. This can be a fun way to get around as long as you don't mind hanging onto a perfect stranger.

Cyclos are another good option for tourists looking to get around. These three-wheeled cycles are ideal for hauling people and cargo as needed around town. You can catch a ride by yourself or with a couple of other people.

Don't bother looking for a taxi in most areas of Cambodia. They are few and far between, so you're much better off taking other forms of local transport.

Outside of the cities, you'll find that most of the transportation options are fairly primitive, but they are a lot of fun. I highly recommend getting a ride in an ox cart at least once. You'll also see carts pulled by horses or buffalo and these all make great memories to tell your family and friends about.

## Long Distance Transport

Trains in Cambodia are freight only. However, it is possible to get on a cargo train if you are willing to pay, though it may be a risk beyond what you want to take. The railway system hasn't been updated in a very long time and derailments are common. It's probably best to stick with other transportation methods.

Buses are probably your best option to get from city to city. The main tourist routes are well paved and offer comfortable, air-conditioned buses to get you where you want to go. Prices are fairly low, too.

If you're feeling particularly daring, hop into a minibus. These pack the passengers in and are driven rather recklessly. You may also catch a ride in a pick-up truck that is headed your way, for a small fee.

## Crossing Water

The entire country is criss-crossed by lakes and rivers, so if you want to travel very far, you'll probably need to cross water. While there are ferries available on some of the larger rivers, they are not the best way to cross if you're looking for adventure.

Take some time and enjoy a boat tour. There are both individuals and companies that can give you a ride and show you the sights before dropping you off at your destination. This is a fun, unique way to travel and is definitely worth doing at least once.

There are no shortages of interesting ways to get from one place to another while you are traveling in Cambodia. The most important thing is to keep your sense of adventure since anything can, and probably will, happen in your travels.

# Cambodia's Food: A Culinary Adventure

As with any country, Cambodia has plenty to offer in the food department. As long as you are willing to try new things, you'll find plenty of affordable places to eat. I feel that food is one of the biggest parts of the culture of a country, so it's important to get out there and try some of it. You'll really miss out if you seek out food you are already accustomed to.

## The Art of Dining Out in Cambodia

As with most countries, Cambodia has specific ways of doing things when it comes to food. When you are eating out, you'll be served your base meal alongside a number of smaller plates. These are usually loaded with peppers, sauces, limes, or herbs that are meant to enhance your dish. These should be used with your meal to create a better flavor.

Also on your table will be a number of very small napkins and a mug of hot water. This is meant for cleaning your utensils, which will be standing in the mug. It's a good way to assure that the pieces are clean, if not completely sterile. Pull out the utensils you need and use the small napkins to wipe the water off before using.

Khmer food is often based on rice and fish, as there are plenty of these to be found in the country. However, the actual cuisine has a wide range of influences. There's a touch of France and China in many of the foods, but Thailand and Vietnam have also affected the direction the food here has taken.

You will definitely want to try amok while in country. This is the national dish and it is made of fish mixed with curry paste and coconut milk, then steamed in banana leaf cups with a little coconut cream on top. This is served in restaurants around the country, so it won't be hard to find.

Grilled seafood is also very popular, particularly in seaside towns, though you'll find grilled freshwater fish in the interior of the country. If you're lucky, the waiter will grill this fresh food right next to your table on a little grill and serve it piping hot with fish sauce, lime juice and cucumbers.

If you're in the mood for something a little heavier, bai sach chrouk is a good option. This is usually served for breakfast. Every restaurant has its own recipe, but all involve slow roasting pork that has been marinated in soy and coconut milk until cooked through. The pork is then sliced and served with rice and a variety of vegetables.

Another tasty option is lort cha, with its soft, fat noodles that are stir fried with a variety of vegetables and soy sauce. They're topped with a runny egg and some chili sauce.

Soups abound in Cambodian cuisine. From kuy teav, a pork broth with noodles and meat, to Muslim beef curry, made with beef and red curry. The latter is served with bread to soak up the delicious broth. Khmer sour soup is a very popular choice among the locals. It's essentially a vegetable stew and is full of easy to find ingredients, including morning glory.

Samlor kako is not for the weak of stomach, but it does hold a special place in the hearts of those living in Cambodia. This national dish contains a number of ingredients, including prahok, fermented fish cheese.

Cambodia is a hot country and you'll find yourself ordering delicious Khmer iced coffee. This is made by roasting coffee beans with butter, then brewing a very rich beverage with is cooled and poured over ice and sweetened condensed milk. It's a caffeine packed sweet drink that will cool you right down.

## Eating On the Street

Any true traveler will tell you that the really good stuff is found on the street. Food, that is. Cambodia is no exception. There are street vendors and little food carts everywhere, both in cities and more rural towns, selling their delicacies for your delight. This food is so cheap that an entire group of travelers can stuff themselves for less than $5 US.

Khao soi is a very popular and filling dish found throughout the country. The dish is a mish mash of meat, pickled cabbage and egg noodles, which have been boiled and fried so that some of the noodles are crunchy. There are plenty of fresh herbs added to the broth to give it a delicious flavor.

Many street vendors offer individual ingredients as well, which you can purchase and add to rice or a baguette. Baguettes are a remnant of the French occupation and are still prevalent everywhere in the country. Try twa ko, a delicious sausage full of plenty of fat. Some people even make it with pork belly and the smell of this being fried up is mouthwatering. Bai sach chrouk is a nice simple dish, made with cracked rice and coconut milk marinated pork that is grilled and added to broth.

Lok lak is another nice, simple dish for when you don't want a ton of flavor. Beef cubes are cooked and tossed with salad and red onions. There's a nice, spicy sauce to go with it, which you can skip if you desire something a little simpler.

Another light dish that is just as fun to purchase, as it is to eat is nom banh chok, more commonly referred to as Khmer noodles. Women carry baskets of ingredients and walk along the street. When you buy from them, the women will unpack all their ingredients and scoop thin rice noodles from one basket and toss it with a variety of raw vegetables and fish curry.

If you fancy a little snack, the street vendors won't disappoint. From unripe mangos, guava, jujube and other fruits served with a sugar, chili and salt powder to sprinkle over it, to deep fried or grilled bananas served on skewers, there's something for every taste.

Still want something sweet? Try an ice cream sandwich, which is literally coconut ice cream scooped into a dinner roll, or num sang khya l'peou, a custard made of coconut milk, egg and palm sugar, baked inside a hollowed out squash. This pumpkin custard is served in slices, with ice and coconut milk on top.

Burnt sugar donuts are another dessert-like snack. They are not much like donuts except they're round with a hole in the middle, but the burnt sugar topping makes them delectable. Look for Khmer cakes, as well. These small bites are made with taro and mung beans, usually with some candied fruit on top.

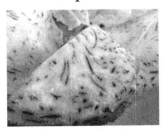

Speaking of taro, watch for taro chips. Most vendors fry them up and then cover them with sesame seeds. Apart from the frying, these could be considered a pretty healthy snack.

If you are in Siem Reap, watch for sticky rice stalls near the rice paddies. These offer sections of bamboo with rice and beans or rice and mango in them. You buy the chunk of bamboo and break off a piece to use as a spoon. They also include coconut milk with the sticky rice, so the entire mixture is rather sweet and delicious.

Num kachay or chive cakes, num pang pate or pate sandwiches and fried noodles, also called mi char are all great snacks, as well. In the Old Market in Siem Reap, you'll find dried mango and nuts that can be handy for day excursions to the temples. Spring rolls also abound, both fresh and fried.

Dried and fresh fish are also abundant, as well as all types of seafood, grilled or fried and served with rice or noodles. Keep your eyes open and you'll find that there are plenty of appetizing foods around.

Depending on where you are, you may find a few more exotic snacks around, as well. These include things like snakes on skewers, roasted over an open fire and served up with tasty sauces, and insects of all types.

To quench your thirst, buy a soda or bottled water from the small shops that are found everywhere, or you can look for coconut water vendors who will cut open a green coconut and pour the water into a bag for you to drink. This is worth trying at least once.

## Hit the Market!

The markets in Cambodia are a fun place to visit, especially if you are planning on trying some of the food you'll find there. Fresh fruit and vegetables abound, so if you have a kitchen or just a place to wash and slice things, you can make your own meals very cheaply.

Fruit can be quite exotic here, including durian, a smelly, yet delicious fruit and rambutan, small round fruit with little spikes that make them look rather alien. Both take a minute to get yourself to try them, but they are both worth a taste.

Of course, coconut, pineapple and papaya are all ever present in the markets, too, so you will want to feast on these as much as possible. There's nothing as good as a very fresh, very ripe mango when you crave something delicious.

While Cambodia definitely has it going on in the food department, there's more to see and do in this beautiful country!

# Must See Sights Around Cambodia

There is quite a bit to see in Cambodia. The country is packed with history and a fascinating place to learn about, so you'll want to check out as many of the historic sites as possible. However, there's even more to visit than just pieces of the past. In a place with such a varied culture, there's plenty to see and do.

## Famous Museums and Cultural Sites

When you're in Cambodia, you'll find that every city has more than enough to keep you busy for weeks. We'll just touch on the highlights, the must-see sights that you really can't miss.

In Phnom Penh, checking out the Royal Palace is something every traveler must do. The palace was built in 1866 and is still in use today. When the King is there, you can't go in, but if he is in one of his other homes, visitors are encouraged. Take a look at the Silver Pagoda while inside. If you want to take a camera in, you'll pay a small fee. Don't forget to walk out in front of the palace, where Sisowath Quay allows for a great view of the river.

When you've finished with the palace, head north and you'll find the National Museum of Cambodia. Built in the early 1900's, the building is traditional and built around a lovely courtyard garden. Within the museum, you'll find some very impressive sculptures. There are four pavilions, each of which covers a specific part of Cambodia's history, from pre-Angkorian art to more modern sculptures. Keep in mind that photos are not permitted inside the museum.

Also in Phnom Penh is the Independence Monument. This huge pagoda shaped monument was built in honor of Cambodia's independence from France. While the independence came about in 1953, the monument was built five years later.

With the rough history that Cambodia has, it's not surprising that many of the important cultural sites refer to the Khmer Rouge. One such place is Tuol Sleng, or S-21, as it was known by Pol Pot's men. This prison was also the execution place for many Cambodians. Here, prisoners were tortured for interrogation before being killed. Everything was meticulously recorded and today, the images they left behind are displayed.

Near Tuol Sleng is a place known as the Killing Fields. The Cheung Ek memorial stands in remembrance of over 17,000 people of all ages who were slaughtered here. The area is full of mass graves and memorial stupa with the bones and skulls of many victims. It is a sad monument, but it is one that every visitor should see so they can better comprehend the horrors of the past.

## Historic Temples and Buildings

One of the most famous places to visit in the country is Angkor Wat. This incredible archeological site spans a good 400 square kilometers, though the temple is only part of the World Heritage site. The Bayon Temple is also located in the park and is full of beautiful sculptures and is one of the top tourist destinations in the country. Built during the 12$^{th}$ century, Angkor Wat is still standing and impressively well preserved. Don't miss the museum where you can see a number of galleries with sculptures and other historic items of interest.

If ancient temples interest you, don't miss the others that are scattered around Cambodia. Wat Phnom was built in 1273 and still stands in Phnom Penh. Angkor Thom is just north of Siem Reap and fairly close to Angkor Wat, so if you're in the area, you should take a look. Built in the 12$^{th}$ century, this was the final Khmer empire capital city.

Other notable temples include Wat Ounalom, which is a little more modern and currently the center of Buddhism in Cambodia, in Phnom Penh. Banteay Kdei, Beng Melea and Preah Khan are just a few of the other sites you may want to visit.

Of course, the country isn't made up entirely of temples and pagodas, though it may seem that way when you start to research them.

## Other Things to See and Do

Dance is a big part of the culture here and you can enjoy it by heading to one of the theaters that features dance performances. Phnom Penh offers outdoor theater at the National Museum, where you can see traditional dances, yike opera and more. In Siem Reap, try Raffles or Nginn Karet Foundation's shows at Wat Bo.

Prefer to have some fun with your learning? Then head to the Cambodian Cultural Village in Siem Reap. This is a unique theme park that is ideal for travelers of all ages. Within the park, you'll find 10 different villages (including a fishing village and a farming village) with famous buildings, local customs and various practices that are common to each area. Dancing is huge here and you'll find plenty of dancing shows, as well as a wax museum and miniatures of the country.

While you're in Siem Reap, take a tuk tuk or free shuttle out to the silk farm. You'll be given a free tour of the mulberry trees used to feed the silk worms and will get to see the whole process of extracting the silk from the cocoons. It's a fascinating visit and you'll have a whole new appreciation for this delicate fabric. Find the shuttle by heading to Artisans D'Angkor in the city. They sell silk products here, which are produced at the silk farm.

Not sure where to go? Ask the locals!

Everywhere you go, you will find yourself surrounded by the rich culture of this country. The people are friendly and more than willing to explain things to the confused traveler so don't be afraid to ask questions.

# Finding Excitement in Cambodia

There's plenty of adrenaline-inducing fun to be had in this country and if you're interested in some excitement, it's not hard to find. It all depends on what you enjoy doing.

## Water Sports

With plenty of rivers and a number of islands in the sea, Cambodia is the perfect place to enjoy some water sports. These include everything from scuba diving to kayaking.

The Kampot River runs through Kampot Province and is just the place to kayak and enjoy the jungle and tiny villages. The river gives you plenty of calm moments, but there are rapids, as well. You can stop wherever you like along the way and explore the shoreline a little more, as well.

Surfing is minimal along the coastline, thanks to calm waters, but if you head out of Sihanoukville to Bamboo Island, the beaches there see some decent waves. Just make sure you have your board with you, since there are no rentals available on this secluded island. You can also go windsurfing off the coast.

For diving, head to Sihanoukville, a small town on the coast. There are several diving schools here, so anyone can enjoy the area. You'll be diving around the little islands that are just off the coast. There are plenty of reefs available to look at, but you might enjoy Sting Ray Alley. Don't forget to ask about night dives, too.

## Land-based Fun

Even if you're not into water, you can have a blast here. Head to Siem Reap and visit the Angkor Archaeological Park where you can fly through the jungle on Flight of the Gibbon. This amazing zip line begins 80 meters in the air, so you're far above the trees and temples. There are ten zip lines in total, including a tandem line. If you're not as interested in zipping, you can still get a bird's eye view on one of the four sky bridges that take you right through the forest.

If you're in the town of Sihanoukville, on the coast, take a tuk tuk to iball Adventure Park just outside of town. This park offers a zip line across a lake and a rockpool for swimming. The real attraction here is the iball downhill run, however. You are put inside an inflated ball and then rolled down the hill. It's a rough and tumble adventure, certainly worth trying once.

Enjoy rock climbing? There are a few areas where you can climb around the country. Take a tour with <u>Climbodia</u> and you'll be guided through caves and terrain to find the best places to scale the rocks.

For a truly unique experience, try firing off an AK-47 or an M16 at Phnom Penh's shooting range. It's located inside a military base, but if you're heading in to shoot, you can pass right on through. They also allow visitors to throw hand grenades and shoot off bigger guns, for a fee. It's a bit pricey, but probably the only time you'll ever hold a real rocket launcher!

There's more than enough to keep you busy around Cambodia. Whether you want to enjoy the water, land or sky, there's something for everyone here. Including great places to hang out all night if you're into partying.

# Nightlife in Cambodia's Top Cities

Nightlife is non-existant in many of the smaller towns in Cambodia, but if you're in Siem Reap, Phnom Penh or Sihanoukville, you'll find there are some crowds out in the evening. Imported beer is available just about everywhere, so you can find a wide range of beers to try in any bar in the cities.

In Siem Reap, head to Pub Street after nightfall to find plenty of bars. Most regular restaurants that serve alcohol will close around midnight. Actual bars, however, can stay open as late as they wish, so some are open 24 hours a day. Bugs Café is an interesting place where you can drink and dine on . . . insects. It's not for the weak of stomach. More traditional bar fare can be found at Charlie's, Mezze, or Island Bar.

Most happy hours start at 4 pm and run for a couple of hours, so if you're looking to save money, this is the best time to drink. In Phnom Penh, try The Empire for a classy bar with a range of international food served. There is a little theater upstairs that serves food and drink while you watch a movie, as well. California Hotel is another good option for 24 hour drinking, while Angry Birds Bar is a hopping bar and nightclub in Phnom Penh that draws tourists and locals alike.

Outside of the capital city, you might want to try Here Be Dragons in Battambang or the After Work Pub in Sihanoukville.

## Partying It Up at the Casino

While Westerners may head for the bars and nightclubs, Asian tourists and business people tent to head to the casinos that are so prevalent in Phnom Penh and Siem Reap. Gambling is a big deal here, but it's not usually for the broke backpackers, as one play in the casino can cost more than your food for a whole weekend.

That being said, casinos can be a fun place to listen to live music and enjoy drinking. In Phnom Penh, Nagaworld is the big place to visit, with live concerts every night and plenty of gambling to be done. There are two main casinos here, so you can choose where you want to spend your time. In Siem Reap, Lucky Diamond is the place to be. It's smaller than Nagaworld, but still worthy of a visit if that's your thing.

Whether you are interested in drinking a beer with some friends, dancing or just playing some blackjack, the bigger cities in Cambodia can accommodate you. There is plenty to enjoy while you're out and about.

# Your Cambodia Bucket List

Cambodia is a pretty amazing country to explore, but if you are short on time, here are a few things that you absolutely must see in each city you visit.

## Siem Reap

Siem Reap is one of the cities every visitor should enjoy. It is near a large number of temples, including Angkor Wat.

**1. Learn to cook Cambodian food.** Take a cooking class at Le Tigre de Papier, a renowned restaurant in the area.

**2. Visit the lotus farm.** Just outside of the city, you'll find a beautiful farm where lotus flowers are grown. You can even take part.

**3. Check out Angkor Wat.** If you've come this far, you must see the ancient temple for yourself.

**4. Take a motorcycle tour.** Get up close and personal with the jungle and villages surrounding Siem Reap via motorcycle.

**5. Tour the Cambodian Cultural Village.** This theme park will tell you all you need to know about the culture in this country.

## Battambang

This quiet area is home to many rice paddies and is a tranquil, beautiful place to visit.

**1. Take a ride on the bamboo train.** This unique journey on a Norrie, or bamboo mat may look dangerous, but it's fairly safe and is a fun way to travel for a short while.

**2. Visit the winery.** There is a small winery just outside of Battambang and while the wine isn't terrific, the juices are great and the owners very entertaining.

**3. Walk around the temples.** Battambang has several temples to enjoy, including Phnom Banan and Wat Baset.

## Kompong Cham

This little town is definitely worth visiting. The architecture here is French Colonial and very different from other areas in Cambodia. It is also home to Cham or Chinese Muslims who have made their home here.

**1. Climb the French Watchtower.** This tower would warn the Governor of danger by lighting a fire at the top.

**2. Visit Prey Chung Kran Weaving Village.** This village is where you can find exquisite, hand woven cloth and see how it is made before purchasing.

**3. Cross the bamboo bridge to Ko Paen.** This island is only accessible by boat for part of the year, but during the dry season, you can walk across a bamboo bridge to reach it.

## Phnom Penh

Phnom Penh is the capital city of Cambodia and is home to many of the more important, modern sights here.

**1. Walk along Sisowath Quay.** This historic quay runs in front of the Royal Palace, which is also a must see.

**2. See a Kun Khmer match.** Head to the TV station hosting a Khmer kickboxing match and you can watch for free.

**3. Pick up souvenirs on Koh Dach.** This handicraft island is in the middle of Mekong River, not far from Phnom Penh. Buy some goodies and relax on the beach.

**4. Immerse yourself in the past.** First, head to Tuol Sleng, which was an extermination center for the Khmer Rouge. Then visit the Killing Fields for a more complete experience.

**5. Visit the Night Market.** Pick up some souvenirs in a more relaxed environment on weekends from 5-midnight at Preah Mohaksat Treiyani Kossamak .

# Final Words

I hope you've enjoyed reading and learning more about Cambodia. I also hope that it has inspired you to visit this gorgeous country and experience the wonder of its culture for yourself.

While this guide is relatively short, it should give you all the basic information you need to go to the country and enjoy traveling around. Cambodia has a lot to offer the visitor who is truly interested in learning more about the tough history and amazing resilience found here.

Chances are, once you arrive in Cambodia, you'll find yourself drifting off the beaten track and enjoying rural villages and new experiences. Just don't wander into any potential minefields and you'll be fine. Try everything once and you will have stories to tell your grandchildren!

If you get stuck, the Khmer are a friendly people and more than happy to help you out. Just ask if you need a hand and you'll see the friendliness first hand.

Finally, if you enjoyed this book, I'd love a review on the book. If you can take out 5 minutes of your time and let other readers and me know how it helped you, it would be very appreciated. Your fellow readers will be thankful to know what to expect and I'll be able to continue to improve my travel guide series.

## Tom Yung Goong

This soup is one that every visitor to Thailand must try. It really sums up the incredible flavors found here. With lemongrass, kaffir lime leaves, galangal and chilies, the soup is particularly tasty. You'll find assorted vegetables and shrimp floating in the elegant broth, as well.

## Gaeng Som

Best known as sour soup in English, you should try ordering this throughout Thailand, as ever region has its own style. In Bangkok, the soup is sweet and sour and contains shrimp, while ordering the same thing in southern regions will get you a chili and turmeric broth.

## Geang Keow Wan Gai

Thai green curry is a very popular dish and for good reason, it's delicious. This particular dish is a comfort food in Thailand and is usually served with steamed rice. The coconut milk, chicken, eggplant and chilies all combine to make a truly amazing meal.

## Tom Saap

Tom Saap is a traditional Isaan soup and is best eaten in this region. It contains the usual herbs, lemongrass, kaffir lime leaves and galangal, along with plenty of peppers and mushrooms.

## Gai Pad Pongali

Yellow curry may not be as common as Green curry in Thailand, but it is still used. Any kind of meat can be used and cooked in the yellow curry. In this particular dish, eggs are used to create a more filling plate of chilies and veggies. However you'll probably want to try the crab version that is available around Bangkok.

## Gaen Tai Pla

When in the south of Thailand, try ordering this fish stew. It is a delightful mix of salt and heat and is full of bamboo shoots, beans and carrots to fill you up. The real flavor comes from grill fish kidneys.

## Hor Mok Ma Prow Awn

Here is a unique dish that will appeal to just about everyone. The seafood curry is cooked in a pan with coconut cream and then served inside a coconut. It is a delight to the senses and has just a hint of sweetness from the young coconuts that are used.

## Joke

Joke is usually served in the early morning, as breakfast. It's not remotely sweet, however. Joke is actually rice porridge that is cooked with meat broth (usually pork) and served with bits of ginger and onions or an egg in the center of the bowl.

## Pad Sataw

You might be a little leery of eating something known as stink bean, but this dish is actually really good. The beans are similar in texture and flavor to peas and hold their own in this dish that is most commonly served with shrimp or pork.

## Mookata

Traditionally served as a Street food, mookata has made the transition to restaurant. You will be given a little grill for your own use and you can cook up as much as you want for your lunch or dinner. It's a unique barbecue experience that will give you memories to last a lifetime.

## Hoy Tod

Omelets range from simple to complex and hoy tod is definitely on the more complex side of things. While it is often referred to as fried oysters, the oysters are in an omelet, served atop bean sprouts with cilantro. In seafood restaurants you can order a version that includes tomato sauce.

## Street Food

Street food is definitely a good way to experience the local culinary culture and Thailand's street food is very affordable. However, you should take steps to ensure you don't get sick. Look for street carts that have plenty of people eating there and look for fresh food, as opposed to food that has been sitting out for a long while, particularly seafood. With a little common sense, you can enjoy the flavors without any side effects.

## Kai Yang

Kai yang is basically grilled chicken, but it is nothing like Western chicken. The Thai tradition is to use garlic, pepper, fish sauce and coriander root that is rubbed into the poultry before it is grilled. There are usually a few sauces to choose from, as well. You will find this delicious street food in Isaan.

## Satay

One of the most iconic dishes in the country is satay. There are several types, depending on the meat used. Pork is most common, but you will also find chicken and very occasionally beef satay, as well. The meat is marinated in a mixture of coconut milk and turmeric, then skewered and grilled. Peanut sauce is used for dipping and pickled vegetables are often served with the meat.

## Som Tam

Som tam is often served with other foods as a side dish. It is a salad made from green papaya and beans. It usually includes tomatoes, dried shrimp and peanuts, as well as chilies. The spices are usually muddled with a mortar and pestle and then mixed into the salad. You can also find variations that include fermented crabs, oysters or fish.

## Pad Kee Mao

If you translate pad kee mao, it actually means drunken noodles. This is a fitting name since the dish is just the thing after you've been drinking. The noodles are wide and fried with veggies and a few different meats in a big mixture of tasty, greasy goodness.

## Hot Pot

This classic meal can be eaten in a restaurant or in the street. You'll be given a clay pot of boiling broth where you can drop in your own vegetables. Spice up the soup a little with eggs, pork or bean thread noodles and share with some friends.

## Mango Sticky Rice

Mangoes are tasty on their own, but when they are sliced and arranged on top of sticky rice, then drenched in coconut milk, they are divine. This is the one dessert that everyone needs to try while in Thailand. Even if you aren't a big fan of mangoes, you will probably enjoy this simple dessert.

## Kai Yad Sai

Another popular dish on the street is this stuffed omelet. These are a delicacy that is rarely found elsewhere and certainly not in sit-down restaurants. The egg is carefully fried, then gathered up around a filling of pork mince with vegetables and a nice, tangy sauce. Add a plate of steamed rice and you have a simple, yet nourishing meal.

## Khao Neow Moo Ping

Skewered meat is always a hit as street food and this dish is no different. You'll find the grilled pork on sticks sold with sticky rice that is put into a little plastic bag for you to carry. This is a great snack or a small meal if you're not very hungry.

## Fried Bananas

Although bananas might not sound very exciting, they are an incredible treat when served up fresh out of the hot oil. Ripe bananas are coated in a mixture of coconut and rice flour, then deep fried until golden brown. You can find these throughout Thailand, but usually only street vendors sell them.

## Markets

The Thai markets are not to be missed. You'll love the hustle and bustle of these places, full of noise, smells and sights to dazzle the eyes.

## Lychee

These small, round fruits require peeling before you can eat them. They show up in many Thai dishes, but they're delicious as is. Nibble the translucent flesh off the pit and enjoy the sweetness.

## Mango

Chances are, you've never had a mango as fresh as the ones in the Thai markets. These juicy fruits require a little finesse when peeling and pitting, so you may want to purchase them already cut up. Bring a napkin or wet wipes, since they're very juicy.

## Durian

Looking like a spiky dragon's egg on the outside, durian is one of those rites of passage that every visitor to Southeast Asia needs to pass. The smell is like an open sewer, but the soft yellow flesh is actually divine when you bite into it. Many people never get past the smell, however.

## Longan

Longan is actually related to the lychee fruit and is similar in taste. The brown fruit have a thin, durable shell that must be peeled off to get at the flesh inside. There is a central pit that is inedible, but the rest of the fruit is sweet and light of taste.

## Rambutan

Another alien looking fruit, rambutan is red with hairs sticking out of it. The translucent flesh is sweet and easy to eat, so make sure you get at least a dozen of these. They're delicious and very similar to lychee.

## Jackfruit

Like durian, jackfruit has a somewhat unpleasant smell and a yellow, custardy interior when ripe. The exterior is spiky. It is often eaten while only partially ripe, when the flesh is still crisp. The flavor is sweet and a combination of mango and pear.

## Guava

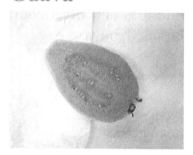

This delicious fruit has many uses and while it may look ordinary and green on the outside, the interior pulp can range from bright pink to white with black seeds. Guava is often eaten raw, but it can also be turned into juice or candied, particularly if it is the sour variety.

## Breadfruit

Breadfruit is related to jackfruit and has a similar spiked rind. Unlike the flavorful jackfruit, however, this one is bland and lacking in flavor. Breadfruit is best eaten in combination with other foods, usually cooked with sauce or spices added to give it a little oomph.

## Mangosteen

You'll see purple round fruits in many of the markets throughout Thailand. When the thick peel is cut open, the center yields a delicious flesh that is both sweet and sour, with apple and pear flavors.

## Tamarind

Tamarind looks somewhat like a bean pod, but the inside contains a sour and slightly sweet fruit that is usually used in paste form. It is added to a number of dishes to add a little tang and while it can be eaten as is, it's a little sour for most people's tastes.

## Dragonfruit

Scaled pink fruit with either white or bright purple flesh, dragon fruit should be on your must-try list. The flesh is speckled with small black seeds, which are edible. It tastes much like a mild kiwi and can be a very enjoyable fruit.

## Noy Naong

These fruits look quite alien, like many of the things you'll find in the market. They are green and scaled, in the shape of a rounded heart and also known as custard apples. Inside the fruit, white flesh is studded with black seeds. Eat it with a spoon and enjoy the pear pudding flavor.

Made in the USA
Las Vegas, NV
15 October 2024

96892054R00077